ROOTS PUNK

American Made Music Series

Advisory Board

David Evans, General Editor
Barry Jean Ancelet
Edward A. Berlin
Joyce J. Bolden
Rob Bowman
Curtis Ellison
William Ferris
John Edward Hasse
Kip Lornell
Bill Malone
Eddie S. Meadows
Manuel H. Peña
Wayne D. Shirley
Robert Walser

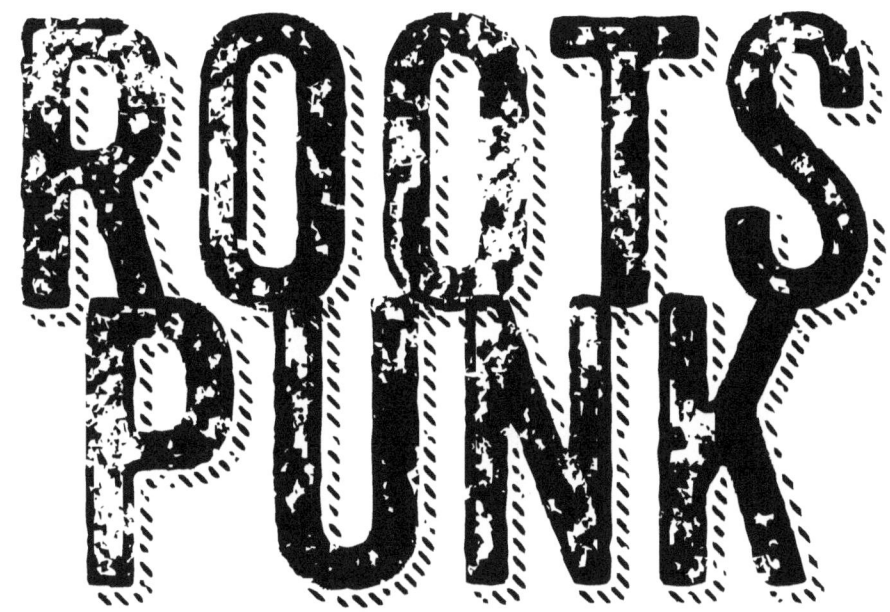

ROOTS PUNK

A Visual and Oral History

David A. Ensminger

University Press of Mississippi / Jackson

The University Press of Mississippi is the scholarly publishing agency of the Mississippi Institutions of Higher Learning: Alcorn State University, Delta State University, Jackson State University, Mississippi State University, Mississippi University for Women, Mississippi Valley State University, University of Mississippi, and University of Southern Mississippi.

www.upress.state.ms.us

The University Press of Mississippi is a member of the Association of University Presses.

Copyright © 2023 by University Press of Mississippi
All rights reserved
∞

Library of Congress Cataloging-in-Publication Data

Names: Ensminger, David A., author.
Title: Roots punk : a visual and oral history / David A. Ensminger.
Other titles: American made music series.
Description: Jackson : University Press of Mississippi, 2023. | Series: American made music series | Includes bibliographical references and index.
Identifiers: LCCN 2023028651 (print) | LCCN 2023028652 (ebook) | ISBN 9781496848413 (hardback) | ISBN 9781496848420 (trade paperback) | ISBN 9781496848437 (epub) | ISBN 9781496848444 (epub) | ISBN 9781496848451 (pdf) | ISBN 9781496848468 (pdf)
Subjects: LCSH: Punk rock music—United States—History and criticism. | Punk rock musicians—United States—Interviews. | Americana (Music)—History and criticism. | Cowpunk music—History and criticism. | Hardcore (Music)—History and criticism.
Classification: LCC ML3534.3 .E6505 2023 (print) | LCC ML3534.3 (ebook) | DDC 781.660973—dc23/eng/20230707
LC record available at https://lccn.loc.gov/2023028651
LC ebook record available at https://lccn.loc.gov/2023028652

British Library Cataloging-in-Publication Data available

Julie Ensminger
Our first weekend, a shared enthusiasm for Jason and the Scorchers,
and a marriage often built around the love of music

Laura Patterson/Ensminger
For spinning *Miami* by the Gun Club hundreds of times

Prof. Daniel Wojcik
For showing me the path, again and again,
from our mutual punk origins to endless possibilities

Special thanks to:
Edward Colver, for the use of select photography from his stellar vault

Edward Colver, Los Angeles, CA, 2021, by David A. Ensminger.

CONTENTS

3	1. Roots Punk, a Reckoning
31	2. The Blasters: They Play American Music
45	3. Elvis vs. El Vez
65	4. Gary Floyd: Heart and Mind with the Power of a Freight Train
77	5. Dave Dictor: My Story Is a Little Weird
89	6. Jeffrey Lee Pierce: Ghost on the Highway
107	7. Texacala Jones: Oh Mother
119	8. Chris Desjardins: A Hard Road to Follow
129	9. Rank and File: The Conductor Wore Black
137	10. Peter Case: Beyond the Midnight Broadcast
153	11. Alejandro Escovedo: A Man of Certain Influence
159	12. Mike Watt: Portrait of the Artist as a Bass Man
171	13. The Hickoids: Harness the Corn Demon
179	14. The Beatnigs: When You Wake Up in the Morning
185	15. X: Under the Big Black Moon
199	References
203	Index

ROOTS PUNK

1
ROOTS PUNK, A RECKONING

*I*n the mid-1970s, pop music's hold on culture loosened as unruly young music makers punctured the ongoing output of feelgood fizzy hits that Jello Biafra, singer for the Dead Kennedys, dubbed "schlocky music . . . whole-wheat fluff" for the baby boom, vid-kid, post–atom bomb generation (qtd. in Vale). Chartbusters of the era included Wings, ABBA, Leo Sayer, and Starland Vocal Band, whose dominance began to fissure under the duress of new music. Perhaps most incendiary were the Sex Pistols, caricatured in 1977 as "the foremost incisors in the slavering maw of London's rabid punk-rock scene . . . vaguely anarchistic, willingly antagonistic, the droogs . . . of the dangerously uncivilized age prophesized by *A Clockwork Orange*. They've got no class, and they've got no principle of the traditional sort" (Demorest 30–31). This was the period of visible unrest, dissent, and challenge to norms.

Although punk gained steam, first in the UK and then in the United States, especially rippling through DIY fanzine networks, college radio markets, and indie record shops, the genre did not become omnipresent and widespread within mainstream culture until the likes of Green Day and Nirvana in the 1990s. In 1977, the press bathed their punk coverage with descriptions such as "they resemble Romulans . . . the crazies shave their skulls like survivors of lobotomy operations . . . the mob twitches to an electrified bunny hop in a dim cellar" (Demorest 32). And, as Stiv Bators told *Trouser Press* in 1983, "the media manipulated it to make [punk] look violent and now punk's dead" (qtd. in Young 17). Indeed, the violence police inflicted upon the punk scene—batons, police helicopters, gauntlets of squad cars—forced fifty-six clubs that catered to such crowds to close down around 1983, according to the *LA Times*. Yet the genre endured and grew even more "hardcore."

Originally, before the wooing and woeful melodies of mall-friendly pop-punk like the Ataris, punk offered scathing, stark bluntness rather than succulence; bitterness rather than banality; rapid and fragmented narratives rather than dreamy indulgence. It was phlegm instead of fop; gunk rather than glitter; street rhetoric rather than sagas. It brimmed with caustic and haphazard outbursts rather than music defined by skilled dexterity. Instead of teenybopper, it was fanged and tattered. As Rob Younger, singer of Radio Birdman, intoned to me: "Simplicity, directness, good songwriting and attitude doesn't require a traveling circus to support it . . . the power of ideas, of art, isn't, or shouldn't be, dependent on extravagance and over-embellishment" (8). Or, in a more incendiary approach, the Weirdos sang, "Broke all my records and my stereo / Ripped up my tickets to see ELO / I say, destroy all music."

Yet punk, despite the commonly used rhetoric about throwing away the past or colliding with it head-on, was often an expression of continuity, a convergence with personal histories, varied cultural heritages, a sense of regionalism, whether Colombian and South African, Scottish and Welsh, Los Angeles and New York, and musical manifestations of all stripes. Though the notion conjures up images of Johnny Cash in steel-toed Dr. Martens boots, roots punk does not simply mean delivering past styles—like traditional folk, country, or blues chord progressions and storylines—onto punk modes and manners. It certainly can be, but it is also about a frame of mind, a looking glass into an artist's obsessions and compulsions, in which the past is woven into the present, including idiosyncrasies that have shaped personal taste, manners, and style. And this entire book delivers a bottom-up, interview-intensive approach. This is not a theory-driven analysis: these are a series of conversations, an act of listening, in which the artists speak for themselves, mostly. It does not lessen the complicated nuances of punk, or smooth its edges: it provides depth and provenance. As Mike Watt of Minutemen told me, "Life puts you in trippy places to learn lessons—IF your mind is open enough to receive it." To keep the book rather organic, I try to relay and telegraph artists' input with little reshaping or authorial intrusion when feasible, much like the Conversations with Filmmakers Series in the catalog of University Press of Mississippi.

Indeed, punk itself was imbued with a striking and continuous crossbreed of musical forms. It cast a wide web, pulling in listeners who might first inaugurate their ears with Elvis Costello, Ian Dury, Squeeze, and the Police and

Jack Grisham, TSOL, Fitzgeralds, Houston, TX, 2014, by David A. Ensminger.

then discover more shambolic, edgier, or more gritty bands like Eater, Stiff Little Fingers, and Killing Joke.

As Jack Grisham, singer for TSOL, recalls: "When we started out, Elvis Costello was punk. I mean, the Go-Go's were punk. There was a lot of stuff like that which was considered punk rock. It was different, because back then it was in the attitude, instead of the music. I mean the music was cutting edge or whatever, more experimental, but it was mainly the attitude. Now, there's the music and the look, but there's no attitude to it. There's nothing that truly makes it punk rock." Those acts were like stepping stones.

As TSOL guitarist Ron Emory tells: "I wasn't really into music, ever. I was into surfing and skating, that's it. Then sometime in 1978 the Dickies and Weirdos played a couple blocks from my house, there were Elvis Costello and Joe Jackson, like we were mentioning. There were all these bands, and I kept going to shows. It seemed like every weekend you were going somewhere. And standing there watching these guys, I thought, I could do that. I worked a job in a parking lot until I could buy a guitar, then I quit. I bought my first guitar, and just tried to do what they did."

Punk broke the mold, at least partially. It meant that everyday people—the musically illiterate and low-life, those (like the early Germs) who could barely scratch or eke out a note on a battered guitar—could shift their lives from being mere consumers to being makers. It grew out of the residual style, musical mischief, lore, and attitude of bands ranging from MC5, the Stooges, Velvet Underground, New York Dolls, and Jonathan Richman to garage bands aplenty, the so-called *Nuggets* sound including the Sonics, Chocolate Watch Band, Love, the Troggs, the Music Machine, Count V, Larry and the Blue Notes, and 13th Floor Elevators. This side of the punk equation inspired entire labels with retro-fuzz tendencies: Midnight Records, Big Beat, Crypt Records, Get Hip Records, Voxx, and Dionysus Records. The latter's advertising featured quotes from critics fawning over bands with descriptions like: "Raving Mad! Psychotic Ramblings from Four ugly lunatics . . . Pure Primitive Rock-n-Roll . . . FUZZ, THUD, and a lot of NOISE!"

Such raw descriptions fit bands aplenty, from early Dwarves, Hysteric Narcotics, Yard Trauma, the Unknowns, the Shakin' Pyramids, Mad Daddys, Plan 9, the Pandoras, early Bangles, and Lyres to Chesterfield Kings, Deja Voodoo, Snake-Out, Thee Hypnotics, the Delmonas, Lime Spiders, Droogs, Fuzztones, the Cynics, the Gories, the Stems, Billy Childish projects, the StingRays, and many more. To understand that underbelly of the punk rock experience, Lee Joseph, whose imprint Dionysus and Bacchus Archives helped keep much of the garage punk genre available, noted to me: "The original punk rockers were all born in the fifties and were raised during a great era of rock 'n' roll. We all saw it coming crashing down in the seventies. Punk created a bridge that bypassed all the excess of seventies arena-rock and singer-songwriter boredom . . . I think that almost every punk band and proto-punk band from the seventies either covered or acknowledged the great (and one-hit wonder) bands of the sixties . . . the simplicity of the songwriting, the aggressiveness . . . the anti-authoritarian attitude" (17). Punk was the means by which to channel and convert those catalytic energies on stage and screen.

Tequila Mockingbird was omnipresent in the early 1980s, both as a singer and a producer for *New Wave Theater*, a UHF television program that featured live countercultural bands like Angry Samoans and the Plugz, which aired on Channel 18 in the Los Angeles region. Now, as a historian, occasional lecturer at UCLA and University of California, Riverside, as well as a founder of the Punk Museum in Los Angeles, she is a fluid anchor to the past who provides, as she calls it, a quick primer:

"I don't think that *New Wave Theatre* got any credit because when Peter Ivers [murdered host of the show, noted harp player who gigged alongside New York Dolls, and musician who scored the cult favorite *Eraserhead*] was killed, it was such an ugly mess. The director swept it under the rug and quickly started something called *The Top*, but I would not work with him anymore because he used to pull guns on me and Peter all the time. He was a really crazy person. Richard Skidmore and myself are Do Monkey Productions, and we went out and hit three clubs a night for three years just to get enough talent to get on the show. We shot every Saturday. We would put six bands in a circle, like a clock, and shoot all the bands just by moving them into position because the cameras were too heavy to move around, so the bands were actually easier to move instead.

"I love what we shot: X, 45 Grave, Castration Squad's 'No Mercy for the Dead,' Vox Pop's 'Just Like Your Mom.' We had lots of cool stuff. Blasters. The Go-Go's. Black Flag. Circle Jerks. All first incarnations—1980–83. I think we were part of Hollywood too. I think that people saw kids jumping all over the place, jumping all over each other. Stage-diving really started to happen on our TV show. I am not saying we were the first, I am saying the first I knew of it was at our show.

"Those same energies attracted a Hollywood guest knee-deep in his own troubles: "By the time that Fear got onto *Saturday Night Live*, we had John Belushi coming to *New Wave Theatre*. We could not get rid of him. He was busy wanting to be a punk rocker and hanging out on set all the time. Peter knew all the people from *Saturday Night Live*. He was part of the Bostonian Harvard crew. It was like brains vs. brawn. He was super-intelligent. With his death went the intelligence, I am telling you. The top was Dan Aykroyd and Chevy Chase, and they came out on stage and made fun of punk rock in front of Fear. Then, bass player Derf Scratch kicked them in the balls, and that was the end of the TV show."

And the end of an era.

So, if some bands worked their way backwards from punk and hardcore to the 1960s garage milieu, that did not occur by accident. "Every novelty runs its course," Gregg Turner, guitarist and singer for the Angry Samoans, told me. "The three or four years centering around the release of *Back from Samoa* became suffocating pretty quick. I mean, seeing 200 kids erupt when we'd launch into 'Lights Out' with white plastic forks making spastic eyeball impalement gestures for all eighty seconds as it played out live was invigorating the first few times around. Then I felt like I was part of Sha Na Na [bad

American doo-wop group from the 1970s/1980s] going thru the motions of invective as a cartoon figure. It was all so expected and staged—there was nothing left to be appalled at. So, reworking the original 1960s proclivities (Mike and I were essentially connoisseurs of vile garage band workouts from the 1960s) seemed like the only alternative to invigorate. What came out in the form of *Yesterday Started Tomorrow . . .* and *STP* were, maybe, hybrids of this and the 1980s trappings we'd been stuck with (at that point in time)" (*Left of the Dial* 20–21).

Such junctures illustrated the band's musical trajectory back in space and time to Roky Erickson and the 13th Floor Elevators, Gerry Roslie of the Sonics, Jim Sohns of the Shadows of Knight, or Dave Aguilar of the Chocolate Watch Band, who deeply impressed Turner because "they weren't faking it. The psychosis they were dishing out was from the soul" (qtd. in Stegall 20), not the result of an affectation or mask meant to impress disenchanted and alienated punks. Turner was keen on those who embodied unkempt, transgressive emotional states of being and a primordial, atavistic rock 'n' roll sense of musical decontrol.

As Michael Stewart Foley, author of the 33 1/3 Series book exploring *Fresh Fruit for Rotting Vegetables* by the Dead Kennedys, explained to me in the *Houston Press*: ". . . the median age of punks in 1978 was twenty years old. That means that most of them grew up listening to early rock and roll, R&B (that is, the real, original R&B that grew out of blues, jazz, and gospel), rockabilly, and country. No small number of them . . . were obsessive record collectors, saving every cent they could to spend on music. For all we hear about the importance of the Stooges, Velvet Underground, MC5, New York Dolls to every kid who became a punk, there's almost always a much deeper, more varied musical history in every punk's story. When I do oral history interviews with punks, I start by asking them to tell me about their lives pre-punk: about their parents' work, politics, religion, etc., but also about what kind of music they were hearing from an early age, what resonated with them. And no matter what, these were American kids listening to American and British rock and roll, so, at most, we're only ever a few steps away from the blues."

Punk as an adjective was often meant to convey a certain anarchic kick, and as such was loosely applied. A *New York Times* writer described the "puerile-provocative" of a 1977 performance of AC/DC opening for the Dictators at the Palladium, a movie house that morphed into a rock venue, as ". . . the closest thing to the punk norm" (qtd. in Bonomo). But most critics and players draw a direct crayon line to the Ramones as punk paragons.

Minutemen and Angry Samoans. San Fernando Valley, CA, early 1980s.

"On one of my favorite albums of all the times, the first Ramones' album, the music . . . is very simple, but to me it's an artistic simplicity," stressed Tony Kinman, from the Dils, Rank and File, and Cowboy Nation. "That record was cut in the contemporary world of *The Six Wives of Henry VIII* [by Rick Wakeman]. It was cut in the world of Steely Dan, cut in the world of Jethro Tull, in the world of pop music getting ever and ever more complex, and that album was a brilliant intellectual reaction to that." V. Vale, editor of *Search and Destroy*, issued a similar perspective: "This was the age of the 30-minute, horrible, masturbatory guitar solo. There was all this contrivance and artiness in music, and the Ramones brought in a blast . . . with all the fat trimmed away" (qtd. in Stark 68). The Ramones were not solely delinquents from Queens mouthing hooligan lyrics about glue, loudmouths, and beating on brats, as well as reckless Nazi references, as some argue, they were serious artists who helped steer a new course in musical history. Hence, the question posed by writer Russell Shaw of *Hit Parader* in his May 1977 Ramones profile title, "But Is This Art?," has been put to rest.

In the punk mode, one day you are "nothing" or invisible, the next you are Joey Ramone, Wayne/Jayne County, Darby Crash or Billy Bones, Poly Styrene or Siouxsie Sioux. And that identity-play and transition happened yet again with the roots punk insurgence, including members of No Alternative, from San Francisco, who morphed from "hardcore punk to punkabilly and rockabilly—Johnny Genocide became Johnny Patterson who's now Johnny Possum" from the Swinging Possums. He declared that "our roots lie in anything from R and B, country, rock, punk, <u>everything</u>—real music. I'm taking something my generation before me did, and applying it to my perspective into the '80s" (Stein).

Looking back and trying to typify punk by giving it guardrails in terms of genre development, or even pretending a unifying theme exists, might border on the futile. "Punk Rock, like so many labels, is misunderstood, mis-defined, etc.," argues Kira Roessler, onetime bass player for Twisted Roots, Black Flag, and Dos. "It was time-specific, audience-specific, and less type-of-music specific." In effect, she is describing a high-context situation—people were committed to modes of dress, coded language use, musical experimentation, do-it-yourself actions from setting up gigs to making, ripping, painting, or repurposing T-shirts and releasing self-made publications—as well as gender bending and norm breaking, whether sexual or political, which can remain remote to outsiders. But Roessler also notes how bands often shrugged off easy categorization: ". . . there were bands at the time which were not appreciated by

Ramones, The Fast and Cool Club. Houston, TX. Mid-1980s.

PUNK GLOBE

JANUARY 1982

In This Issue:
Opel Gardener (A.M.C.) Talks
poet John Cooper Clarke
Punk Globe's 1981 Top Ten

SWINGING POSSUMS wishes all Punk Globe readers a happy 1982!!

punk rock audiences because they didn't conform to preconceptions. Twisted Roots was problematic for those audiences, so were Meat Puppets, Saccharine Trust, and many others. Somehow, the Screamers were okay. It wasn't the instrumentation, though. It was somewhat the style of music. Labels have always sucked, and good bands have always been hard to label."

"The L.A. scene between 1978–1985 was a great music scene because it didn't care about the music industry that much, and it existed on its own, and was an all for one, one for all kind of situation most of the time," explains Dave Alvin of the Blasters. He continues: "For example, the Germs were the first band on Slash; they helped X get on Slash, who helped the Blasters, who helped Los Lobos and Rank and File. Everybody helped each other. It was a social scene that revolved around everyone feeling they were outsiders and didn't fit in. There were negative sides to the scene, like the heavy drugs and alcohol, but everybody did look out for each other and when it died, like all scenes do, I was like a lamb thrown out to the lions. I suddenly realized that just because somebody plays a similar style of music doesn't mean he or she is going to be like everybody back in L.A. There're some real pricks out there, and they're going to screw you over the first chance they get. I miss that about the old L.A. days, and try to carry a little bit of it with me."

In Cerritos, hardcore punk California pioneers Channel 3 themselves felt a strong drift toward roots directions, documented on their album *Airborne*, which featured songs like "True West." Channel 3 guitarist Mike Magrann explains: "I was a big advocate in changing the band's name when we were trying out the new sounds! We were really interested in branching out, and especially liked the opportunity of playing in front of a more diverse (and better looking—hah!) audience. From the tours we did when we were starting to play *Airborne* and beyond songs, we knew the hardcore crowd had no tolerance for listening to any of the new stuff. It felt a hopeless case, to try and convert the punkers to a new sound, to try and attract a wider audience with a hardcore reputation. But hardcore punk was in dire straits around that time, say 1984. The shows were a mess of violence, the majority of big shows ending in riots. Gone were the early melodic days of Southern California punk, we felt, when the early bands were really pushing each other creatively. I guess that's why almost all the Old School punk bands started to branch out and develop.

"Daring to put in a harmonica was a startling new frontier for us," he continues. "As opposed to writing another three-chord banger in 90 seconds, ya know? I think the Enigma [an 'alternative' record label] crew were actually a

Swinging Possums, *Punk Globe*, January 1982.

The Pogues, Pill Labour Club, Newport, Wales, UK.

bit taken aback when we handed in *Airborne*, then *Last Time I Drank*. I mean, they signed us on the reliable strengths of those Posh Boy platters, and another in that vein would've been a solidly reviewed, respectable seller. I think they were aware this new direction under the same name was going to be a tough sell, and they were right! We still stand behind those songs, and unlike a lot of our peers, still play some of them in our set, if only to amuse ourselves. We play 'Last Time I Drank' in the spirit it was conceived, and it sounds more like '77 Clash than anything else. I think the slick production and the trends (hair, boots) maybe made people think we were going heavy metal, when the songs themselves were closer to an earlier U.K. punk sound really. We were actually into a lot of more roots stuff, Creedence Clearwater Revival, Rolling

Next page: The Clash, *Give 'Em Enough Rope* flyer advert, Berkeley, CA.

Stones, Faces. We must've watched *The Last Waltz* weekly! Our songwriting reflected a new freedom, I think. It's almost like the next punkest thing was to branch out, let the songs breathe."

The Pogues, a band that first gestated in inebriated singalongs and merry prankster tuneage filling north London's King Cross pub life, described as an "insalubrious patch of kink, drink and liberty" by *The Guardian*, might be the very definition of roots punk. Their own January 1988 press biography portrays them as "re-animators of the urban acoustic folk style Irish traditional tunes" jolted with "melodic growls and speedy snare drum." They were peers with the Dubliners despite apparent differences, and the Pogues' rowdy and "roughed-up" versions of those icons was "another generation's variations on time-tested trad," as if "singing," according to Shane MacGowan, "an emigrant's memory of what Irish music is like." Their repertoire roiled with pipers, cittern-players, and fiddlers who could easily tap rebel tunes or undiluted, fertile blues, rock 'n' roll, punk attitude, and country cravings.

Meanwhile, when Scream or the Clash dove into reggae, dub, funk, and in the case of the latter, also rockabilly, waltzes, or early hip hop, they were not delivering flimsy facsimiles or copycat style. "These are sources, though," argues Chris Salewicz when discussing the Clash's opus *London Calling*, "not Bowie type steals. There's nothing self-conscious or sneaky about them; it's all out in the open" ("The Clash Play" 18). Also, instead of relying on a few steps of remove—ironic distance and detachment—they were attempting to match and mimic the spirit, not just the grooves, in a way that punk grit and noise alone could not muster. Few punk bands went the length of adding harpsichord, glockenspiel, xylophone, fiddles, and synthesizers as the Clash underwent a musical exploration from dub and gospel to Black-radio friendly funk and well beyond. Such indulgences that saturated the Clash's *Sandinista*, might, however, have been their Achilles' heel. In fact, singer/guitarist Joe Strummer told a *Rolling Stone* writer that the band had, "Wrong turnings, pitfalls along the way . . . We thought we were musicians. Fatal, because you become self-indulgent. Second fatal mistake: 'Hey, I'm an artist.' I'll tell you, Robert Johnson never thought he was an artist."

"Soul music" is how singer Peter Stahl described Scream's version of reggae, including the tune "Still Screaming," which Jamie Rake argued was "the greatest reggae-punk anthem since those days when the Clash meant something" in *Sound Choice* (63) during the mid-1980s. Many, however, might say that premier category belongs to Bad Brains, the all-Black hardcore punk legends from the Washington, DC, area who grafted their nimble, progressive jazz tendencies onto their soulful brand of punk. Stahl framed the convergence this way: "As musicians, lyricists, orators [trying] to get through to people, reggae cuts into the soul much deeper. Everyone can get involved and have something to say. That's why we play reggae" ("Scream"). Though some critics may believe they were using Black music to authenticate their rebellion and rhetoric, or prosper from the plight and hard work of Black musicians, I see a band engrossed in reggae's unique form of communication—its ability to slow down a gig, muster an attention different from the haywire impulse and roughneck reflex of hardcore, and to allow a less destructive sense of dancing and movement.

And in a sense, bands like the Clash were attempting to break down barriers in the perceptions harbored by some of their audience. As bass player Paul Simonon, who grew up amid the heavily Black populations of Ladbroke Grove and Brixton, explains, " . . . we play reggae in our sets and kids come along to the concerts—and some of them are National Front kids—and they like the Clash, and when we play reggae, it's sort of like turning them onto Black music—which sort of helps lead them away from that racist feeling they might have. Which is like changing them" (qtd. in Klein). Absorbing, harnessing, and reimagining Black music became a way to break down the walls of racism. Plus, their rampant tastes for different styles of music can be directly linked to the whims of Joe Strummer as well, who was as smitten by local London acts like funk-soul-ska Hot Point as he was by the older R&B of Little Johnny Jones. "I look for certain sounds," he told *Search and Destroy* No. 6. "I tend to get obscure about it . . . I feel myself going off through a Mexican guitar/cantina phase . . . I'm even hot on Cajun and rockabilly and billarocky, and before that I was into ska and bluebeat" (qtd. in Klein).

"The Clash are exploring all kinds of ideas, going in all kinds of directions, not all of them work, but they were trying dub stuff, funk stuff, they had a go at rap," claims writer Simon Reynolds, author of *Rip It Up and Start Again: Postpunk 1978–1984*, who explained to me: "They did some great things in that period up to and including *Combat Rock*. But it didn't quite register as abrasively modern in the way the post-punk groups did, because the Clash were also doing quite a lot of stuff rooted in traditional American roots music. So, they were exploring the present with their funk/dub/rap tracks but also discovering the richness of the past. Also, they were always, right through it all, a rock 'n' roll band in spirit, and that was what most post-punks were trying to leave behind."

Left behind is the actual cultural context. As Reynolds continued to denote to me: "It does seem quite hard for rock bands to signify in the way that they used to in the sixties and seventies, some kind of disengagement virus has entered the cultural water table. I would say there's even a sense in which white bohemians have 'out-sourced' the burden of building a vibrant counterculture onto Black youth. For some of us, there's a sense in which we've lived vicariously through Black resistance and Black futurism. Which sounds bad, but then, thinking of it another way, why wouldn't someone like myself be drawn to what feels like the most potent, committed, edgy, risk-taking etc. etc. music that's available—i.e., street rap, grime, etc. etc.—especially when the alternative is a whole bunch of wan, not-quite-meaning-it styles of retro-rock?"

Bad Brains, the Ruts, Stiff Little Fingers, the Offs, Toxic Reasons, and even D.O.A. used reggae rhythms, mood, and sentiments. Meanwhile, Velvet Underground's artful swagger and sometimes icy cool, as well as their tunes, were eagerly retrofitted into the sets of Joy Division, the Dils, Eater, Slaughter and the Dogs, and others. Patti Smith herself evoked the gaunt coolness of Keith Richard, and *Grooves* noted her deep influences molded by "the mystical messages of Dylan, Jim Morrison, and Jimi Hendrix," as well as "the overwhelming strength of the Rolling Stones" too (Goldstein 23). But the Avengers recut "Paint it Black" as a fiery single in 1978 and Social Distortion did a blitzkrieg version of "Under My Thumb" during the heyday of California hardcore, as did Scream, from Virginia, at live gigs, who also recorded a version of "Green-Eyed Lady" by Sugarloaf. Los Angeles mavericks X dipped into the catalog of the Doors, Otis Blackwell, the Troggs, and Jerry Lee Lewis, whose film biography *Great Balls of Fire!* featured John Doe as the bass player J. W. Brown.

The Sex Pistols busied themselves with renditions of the Modern Lovers, Alice Cooper, and "Steppin' Stone" by the Monkees, which inspired Washington, DC, hardcore heroes Minor Threat to indulge the tune as well, in addition to covering "12 X U" by art punks Wire and "Sometimes Good Guys Don't Wear White" by the Standells, too (also covered by the Cannibals as well as the Count Bishops). Government Issue, as well as Pure Hell and Splat Cats, re-invented Nancy Sinatra's "These Boots Are Made for Walkin'" for the scuffed combat boots kids, and SOA recharged "Disease" by the UK Subs and dipped into the Monkees' "Steppin' Stone." West Coast surf-punks Agent Orange revisited the Summer of Love with their taut version of "Somebody to Love" by Jefferson Airplane and the Circle Jerks pantomimed Jackie DeShannon's "Put a Little Love in Your Heart"

Channel 3, The Vex, East Los Angeles, CA, 1980s.

and made Garland Jeffreys's observant funk-soul "Wild in the Streets" into a lung-blasting, guitar-overdrive anthem. Hüsker Dü did the same for the *Mary Tyler Moore* theme "Love Is All Around" when the Minnesotans were not resurrecting the Beatles, the Byrds, and Donovan.

Punk has always remained a magnet, pulling elements toward itself, eager to harness and hijack, reimagine and rerecord, bend old chords, melodies, and themes to its own ends. It seeks to sculpt from the highway of music something distinct and borrowed, something blowing in the wind of time past that can be snatched, grabbed, and refitted, used to protest and vent or add satire, ragged luster, and levity to their mania.

A few examples can notably express that. As Jim Kaa of the Crowd told me, his beach-punk band was rife with covers, though not tied to surf music: "We have been doing 'The Kids are Alright' lately. We have done David Bowie, the Weirdos, Magazine, the Yardbirds, Hendrix, Stones, Elvis songs, and more at one time or another." And as *Puncture* reported when John Chandler wrote a review of the Replacements gig at the University of Oregon, the band piled on savage renditions of the "Marines' Hymn" ("From the Halls of Montezuma . . ."), Vanity Fayre's "Hitching a Ride," Bachman-Turner Overdrive's "Takin' Care of Business" (sung with gusto by lead guitarist Bob Stinson), and an impromptu Beach Boys medley ("Help Me Rhonda"/"My GTO")" that proved the gig was not a "genuflecting variety of concert that the inscrutable scribes of the school paper had prophesied" (25). Such a dance with the past often proved to be shambolic and explosive.

As Jason Ringenberg of Jason and the Scorchers, also humorously known as Jerry Lee Rotten, tried to convince me: "I come from the live tradition of Grateful Dead and Bob Dylan in that they are not afraid to do covers. That's great. There are two types of people that do covers: people that do covers because their own material isn't very good and they're a cover act and they don't have their own material, or people that are showing their heritage. I felt that I just wanted to accentuate my own songwriting." Plus, it adds a sense of rootedness to his high-energy performances, which were far more punk than the rest of Nashville. "That character on stage is just the most extreme part of my personality, it's like amplified by 800 percent. Energy just rushes through my personality when I hit stage, so it just comes out. You can't really do something like that thinking about it, it just sort of happens. It's one of the few times in life that I don't have to think about anything. I can just be that thing. The rest of my life I am not like that. I'm a pretty laid-back guy."

Jason and the Scorchers, *East Village Eye*, New York, NY, 1984.

The band was formed when Ringenberg left corn-strewn Illinois, where his hometown Sheffield hosts a monument to the Rock Island Railroad, and anchored himself in Nashville. At the time, rockabilly bands were spawning in England, which he knew would soon infect America as well, so he sought "musicians who had actually grown up on the roots of American music: country and old rock and roll" (qtd. in Gordon 12). Soon, he gathered up guys like guitarist Warner Hodges, who helped forge the blistering "country-punk" combination, and they produced an array of fiery originals and revved-up versions of Carl Perkins and Johnny Cash, that made people love or hate, adore or admonish them. Some simply thought that the band had a kind of "leprosy," like sickened musicians corrupting lauded music. Other critics decried them as a "heavy boogie band with flashy clothes and a new gimmick" whose rendition of "I'm So Lonely I Could Cry" by Hank Williams was "not a credit to old CW legacy, it didn't live up to the punk heritage of the Stooges and Ramones" (Marshall 13). Yet, that slant may be misguided or wrongheaded, for Joey Ramone himself averred, "The guitar player for Jason and the Scorchers said their two biggest influences were us and Hank Williams . . . that makes me happy" (qtd. in Farber 19). That punk idol seemed tickled by the shared sense of legacy.

During their tenure, the Scorchers made Nashville seem . . . edgy, a metropolis of new strains, convergent musical highways, and recombinant history, rather than a yokel place for rehashed riffs or milquetoast country-pop.

Roots Punk, a Reckoning

Jason and the Scorchers, "Golden Ball of Chain," 45 single sleeve, 1986.

"Nashville's got great heritage and history . . . People come to Nashville and don't get what they want out of it, but how many million actors have gone to Los Angeles and never made it?" Ringenberg argues. "Does that mean L.A. doesn't make good movies? How many rock bands went to New York in the 1970s and 1980s and didn't get famous? Does that mean the Ramones aren't valid?" In fact, Ringenberg released the tune "God Bless the Ramones" in 2019. "It's a really silly way of looking at it. On the other side of the coin, you can look at what mostly comes out of Nashville in terms of the money acts, and yeah, it's pretty sickening stuff. But there's still great heritage and a lot of great talent."

A punk band emerging from that cityscape with a blend of New York Dolls and Bob Dylan, Hank Williams Sr. and the Ramones was a feat. Ringenberg continues: "They were guys down in the Lower Broadway section of Nashville, which is now a big money place with NASCAR and Planet Hollywood and places like that, but twenty years ago it was full of seedy, rundown honky tonk places that had been there since the 1940s. All these ancient old bars had all these ancient singers that had sung there every night for thirty years: Curly Putnam, Ray Brand, guys like that who I don't even know if they are alive anymore. They would just sing these songs, maybe there was a single record out twenty years before, and they had these ancient guitars with their names engraved in the neck from some little record deals years before, hair greased back, long sideburns. They made a hell of an impression on a kid from Illinois coming to Nashville and seeing that, and I was seeing it all alone because there was nobody paying any attention. They played for tips to six or seven people. They weren't tourists either. They were down on their luck. Then there were a few kids like me. It was quite inspirational to see those guys sing their lights out and giving their best."

The turning of the tide had arrived, though, and the Scorchers forged not just raw and blazing licks but an attitude that was decidedly and brazenly do-it-yourself, jolted by a punk ethos, despite the odds in a town where slick music was a corporate lifeline. According to Ringenberg: "There was no question at the time that it was a radical thing to be happening in Nashville, a rock 'n' roll band breaking out of there. Nashville was such a little provincial town in those days, a cowtown that happened to have the music business. Country music was all Nashville had at the time. It wasn't like it is now. We didn't come through any of the channels that were set up here. We just made our own channels, we made our own records and put them out ourselves, and heck we had a review in *Rolling Stone* before we even had a record contract. It was pretty exciting times. Everybody was talking about it. Everybody in Nashville knew about the band and was talking about it. Either they loved it or didn't like it, got it or didn't get it, but everybody was interested in it."

And that included *Sounds*, the English music paper, which ran a breathless review, filled with imagined Western slang, of their gig at the Camden Electric Ballroom in May 1985: "Jason yodels through . . . 'I Really Don't Want to Know,' stripping streamers of skin off his larynx . . . All through that steer-chasin' set, in a sweat-wet inferno, Jason kept his handsome ['long red frock coat, purple-lined'] coat on" (Brown 36). After all, he was a man of fashion, not just sheer gusto.

Groundbreaking means that a singer might also form a conduit that leads right back to the origin story. Jason claims: "I think that if I could take any credit for anything in the music business, I can take credit for the fact that I had that unique and original idea, although now it doesn't seem that original. There are a thousand bands doing that kind of thing. But boy I tell you, in the late 1970s and early 1980s, there was maybe two or three [laughs]. I was one of them who had the idea to take roots music and kick the hell out of it. That's why I came to Nashville, to do just that. I think that at times, if Hank came back today, it would be a Scorchers record, if he were in this world today."

And when the Scorchers were covered in *Creem*, the rock 'n' roll cornerstone of writing and fandom, Jason himself notes that the Scorchers had grown and gravitated beyond the guitar-crunch and hectic yowls of their *Reckless Country Soul* EP: "The Scorchers is a real broad-based band, maybe it started out being a country-punk band. I think it has evolved into something that's kind of representative of what's going down in American rock 'n' roll in the last 30 years" (qtd. in Wheeler 20). And in knotting together the firmament of Americana, from its chrome car radio blares to its beer-blotched, stuffed-bar, high-energy guitar salvos in Reagan's era, the band remained true to both the restless spirit of honky-tonkers and Nashville outsiders and punks.

And the band still appeals to a crossover rock and punk audience, including Tony Erba, singer for Face Value, Cheap Tragedies, Fuck You Pay Me, and more: "I love the band. They kind of spearheaded a fresh burgeoning roots/rock thing, a backlash to the tired sequined old country approach. They really shot some electricity into a dead horse and appealed to a younger rock 'n' roll crowd while slathering their songs with biscuit gravy befitting a Waffle House outside of the Hendersonville city limits."

"Roots" and "western" should be understood, then, as something of an umbrella moniker. Invariably, it is meant to signify both figment and fragment of a musical experience, culled from a sense of both locale and lore, enmeshed in songscapes that spill between generations, a manner of singing, conceits of song, turns of phrase, and symbols galore. And, in terms of style, I argue that it connects to a series of genres widely circulated among everyday people in the form of "people's music"—non-elite forms like endless varieties of folk, blue collar rock 'n' roll, non-institutional jazz, earthy blues from porches to roadhouses, and so on. "I always thought the Ramones were folk music, because they played for *folks*, you know? Before they called it country-and-western, they said that Hank Williams was folk music, because it was for the folks, just regular people," argued John Doe of X (qtd. in Willman 31).

Wendy Case, singer and guitarist for the Paybacks, a heavy hitting Detroit tour-de-force, goes a bit further in her view of the convergence. As someone who once lived in the foothills of the Blue Ridge Mountains, exposed to the music of Doc and Merle Watson, Flatt and Scruggs, and Bill Monroe, she believes, "American folk music and punk rock are very similar. They both come from a linear style of storytelling. Simple and direct, not a lot of wanking and wasted notes. It's about getting your message across in the most effective simple manner. And something like the Kossoy Sisters' 'Down In A Willow Garden' is a lot scarier than anything the Sex Pistols ever did."

That connection between Appalachia and the anarchic masses is not lost on Gerry LaFemina, who heads up Savage Mountain Punk Arts. He grew up in NYC in the 1970s and attended punk and hardcore shows at notorious clubs like CBGB, the Peppermint Lounge, and A7 as well as experiencing scenes further regionally afield, such as Pittsburgh, Knoxville, Birmingham, and more. LaFemina, who now teaches at a regional university in Western Maryland, opines: "There's a lot in the roots of Appalachian culture that's at the roots of punk rock. A hardscrabble, get-by-as-you-can, underdog attitude, for one. Secondly, the importance of scene, of community. And let's not forget DIY culture. Long before hipster, artisanal pickle makers landed in Brooklyn, there were guys in beards and overalls making pickles in small towns across Appalachia, listening to outlaw country, speed rock, and punk and doing what they had to do to get by. Anybody could do it. And they often did, particularly as the mines and mills left and they had no other choice.

"Think about it: coal miners' kids gave us punk in England, and punk in Appalachia. And if I look at the bluegrass and roots music community, I see the crossover of musicians (Lucinda Williams producing Jesse Malin, or the current work of Alejandro Escovedo, or the entire X catalog) and similar philosophies. These days, Del McCoury hosts the aptly named DelFest every May in Cumberland, Maryland, for three days of blue grass, traditional, and roots music. Two and half months later, punk acts show up in town for a long weekend of loud-fast rules at the annual Savage Mountain Punk Fest. Half the audience at the former shows up for the latter. Both are run by volunteers. That's punk rock."

Roots punk expresses continuity and change in terms of inherited traditions. The genre is as expansive, varied, nuanced, hybridized, and elastic as punk itself.

Born from mixed Diné (Navajo) and Jewish heritage, the three-piece band Blackfire, with Jeneda Benally on bass and her brothers Klee and Clayson handling the rest, speaks to, and acts on, the issues that endlessly affect Native Americans—the despoiling and encroaching land use by non-natives, genocide and trauma, damaged or constrained tribal sovereignty, ongoing family and substance abuse, and much more. Despite the challenges of engaging two communities at once—indigenous and Western—they have sculpted both a remarkable music catalog and tradition of bearing witness.

Their punk pedigree, unbeknownst to many, is the stuff that most bands dream of, not because they erupted from the Southwest with dynamic, well-oiled grooves and insistent protest music in the land of JFA and Sun City Girls, but because few people have such special links to the Ramones, the godfathers of punk. Jeneda—artist, dancer, model, spokeswoman for the Navajo Nation Tribal Employee Program, and one of the founders of the Indigenous Youth Network—has become an integral part of community consciousness, as have her brothers. Such ethos was profoundly shaped by their father Jones Benally, a medicine man who occasionally joins with them to perform as the Jones Benally Family, in which they honor traditional musical practices and their distinct heritage. They sometimes combine both with punk on gripping tunes, like the title song from their album "[Silence] Is a Weapon," a churning, groove-oriented blast of protest rock that channel both John Trudell (think "Bombs Over Baghdad") and Rage Against the Machine.

Yet, they can also harness the precision and driving thrust of Anti-Flag and Pennywise on tunes like "No Control," in which the husky baritone voice of brother Klee is juxtaposed against Jeneda's higher-pitched backups. On the same album *One Nation Under* (produced by legendary member of Half Japanese, Don Fleming, who also produced Hole, Sonic Youth, and Teenage Fanclub), one can also immerse in Native chants like the Diné Gourd Dance and enjoy the shadowy, submerged presence of Joey Ramone on "What Do You See," one of the last contributions he made before dying. In fact, bassists CJ Ramone (the longtime substitute for Dee Dee Ramone) produced the band's first EP. Blackfire have covered two Ramones songs (as well as Woody Guthrie, too), including their most political jab, "Planet Earth 1988" (featured on *Todos Somos Ramones*), which runs the gamut, critiquing militarism, joblessness, racism, youth crime, drugs, terrorism, and more. While most casual listeners chalk the Ramones up as unserious, bubblegum hooligans, Blackfire saw something far more complicated and meaningful in their repertoire.

On tunes like "It Ain't Over," Blackfire seed mid-paced rock 'n' punk (think Dead Boys meets the Cult's second record) with volatility, heavy crunch, and meditations on the tragedy of compromising freedom in the name of security. Then the speed-soaked "Someone Else's Nightmare" recalls late-1980s hardcore, but with one musical difference and anomaly—a lulling chant in the middle of the fervent barrage. The closest sonic kin might be Beefeater during their *House Burning Down* period. "Stand Strong" is an esteem builder, a call to pride, a way to split the dark clouds, find hope, and persevere against the odds, which have always been stacked unfairly against the self-preservation of First Americans throughout centuries. The fight to protect sacred lands—recently again investigated by the international media when the Dakota pipeline spurred the coalition forces behind Standing Rock Resistance—compels people to protest and persist.

(Silence) Is a Weapon broadened their musical palate to include contributors like Cyril Neville, the funky percussionist/singer behind the Meters, without losing a sense of their swift musical volleys and inveterate conscience, like "Common Ground," which attempts to cut through class, color, creed, and genre. Jeneda's thriving bass complexity and soaring backup vocals return to the fore on "Uprising," a pastiche of revolution rock, homegrown Diné glory, and rhythmic variety, which they move aside for "How Can We Confess." That tune is made from the same vertebrae of much 1990s punk, although they hungrily tackle the issues of gender, class, and sexual preference often missing from the likes of New Found Glory, Senses Fail, My Chemical Romance, and others who played the 2004 Warped Tour with them. Justice comes to those who can afford it, Blackfire avers, as they encourage listeners to resist the "criminalization of dissent" and "stand against the fear and passivity."

Jeneda continues to plug away and tour with brother Clayson in Sihasin, which merges the world of drums and bass (not the genre, literally a two-piece unit) danceability with traditional music, also allowing her vocals to thrive in the forefront with the emotive, cunning, artful uniqueness of someone like Patti Smith (who herself channeled/appropriated Native spiritual music in "Ghost Dance," found on her 1978 platter *Easter*). Some people, though, might prefer Jeneda's tigerish performance on Blackfire's swift breathless cover of "I Believe in Miracles," one of the last seminal cuts by the Ramones.

She has also joined Clayson in extended forays to Native American high schools, which too often suffer dropout rates and youth suicides twice the national average. They teach students how to mold songs, create hope, and find their voice—truly a punk act of conscience fully based on an inveterate and magnetic sense of heritage, place, and identity.

Roots punk should not be bastardized into something like simpleton, sped-up honky-tonk, mock sawdust ballads, or even cow-punk, which gives way to yee-haw caricatures or a marketing gimmick peddled by media. As explains Jeff Smith, front man for the Hickoids, "In the 1980s there was nothing

**Native American Punk Rock
At the WOW Hall on 8th & Lincoln
Saturday, June 12th, at 7pm $5**

convenient about trying to 'market' these 'cow-punk' bands... it was more of an apt 'hat rack' that a lot of incongruous headwear got thrown onto."

Here I try to illuminate that rack even further. This is not a book about how punk was directly shaped by legacies like country, soul, blues, and R&B; for instance, it does not draw an unwavering line between Johnny Cash and Social Distortion. Instead, it is an oral history of sorts, a book that allows the performers to discuss genuine affection for (and sometimes drilling deep into) those genres and cultural milestones, and explores how those genres were soundtracks of their literal roots from a young age onward. That is, it covers roots music, "place" as a symbol and reference point, a lived geography imbued with values and experiences, and roots as a sense of cultural disposition. In doing so, the performers explain, often firsthand, how their own music, lives, and histories emerge woven with a fascination, awe, and commitment to the notes, rhythms, tones, and textures of a motley American milieu.

And although the performers herein tend to cluster around the Los Angeles–Austin axis, that is simply because those scenes are richly interconnected, and I have been involved in both. However, roots-rock bands with punk tendencies could be found everywhere, from Grant and the Geezers in Arizona to Evan Johns in Washington, DC, from Flat Duo Jets in North Carolina to Dash Rip Rock in Louisiana and the polka-punk of Brave Combo in Texas. This book is but a mere sample of the style.

Blackfire at WOW Hall, Eugene, OR.

2

THE BLASTERS
They Play American Music

> Lead guitarist Dave Alvin gave a stirring performance, pounding up and down the stage, wresting song after song out of his guitar. I doubt there wasn't a non-tapping toe in the house by the third song.
>
> —*Ink Disease*, 1983

Raucous rockabilly revivalism swept the globe in the early 1980s like an unrepentant whir of hair pomade and biker grease, though few bands mustered the sheer bravado and earnest dexterity of the Blasters. Many bands plied the genre, like the older generation of Hasil Adkins, Ray Campi, and Charlie Feathers. Upstarts and other acts emerged endlessly too: Levi and the Rockats, Rockin' Rebels, F-Beat, Buzz and the Flyers, Jimmy & the Mustangs, Red Devils, the Funk-A-Billy Rebels (led by Frankie Fix, singer from Crime), Guana Batz, Rockabyes, Tex Rubinowitz and the Bad Boys, Billy Burnette (the son of rockabilly legend Dorsey Burnette), Pink Cadillac, the Morells, Tex and the Saddle Tramps, all female the Stir-Ups, the Blue Cats, and Radium Cats.

Due to the infectious and urgent tunefulness of songs like "Marie Marie," the Blasters deftly navigated rock 'n' roll hot spots, the dive bars of the California farm belt as well as the punk clubs teeming with irate youth donning scruffed, button-strewn leather jackets and combat boots. Portions of this same scene gestated the careers of Dwight Yoakam and Los Lobos. In one gig setting, the Blasters might concentrate on boogie woogie piano, in another on adrenaline and speed. Lead guitarist Dave Alvin's career sprang forward through late-period X (he can be heard on the demos for the album *4th of July*) onto a decades-long solo path. Writer Dave Marsh identifies him with the "heartland vein of John Fogerty, John Mellencamp, and Steve Earle" who focused on telling tales of rogues, workingmen, and people struggling to carve out their lives in uncertain times (34).

"I carry part of Downey, my hometown," Alvin insists: "You could drop me in Antarctica, and I'd still be a Downey guy, even though I haven't lived there

The Blasters, by Edward Colver.

in twenty-something years. With a lot of people, whether they're songwriters, novelists, or painters, you carry those initial memories. My memories of my hometown bring our conversation full circle because it was an area in transition between the rural and urban. It's about 20 miles from LA, and when I was a kid half of it was orange groves, avocado groves, and bean fields. On the south side, there were dairy farms as far as you could see. So, I'm attracted to transitional zones, I'm attracted to borderlands—those places where things collide and people are caught. Usually when I'm writing a song or a poem, those are the images in my head. Something from childhood. I know it sounds loopy, but I think it's true for a lot of writers. They create their own worlds, but they tend to look a lot alike, what they saw when they were young mixed in with what they see now."

Alvin grew up watching bands play at the infamous Ash Grove, situated on Melrose Avenue, guided by owner and operator Ed Pearl. Bands from Buddy Travis to the Limeliters and Lightnin' Hopkins graced the stage, establishing a sense of authenticity and communitas—a spirit of togetherness.

"The common bond between my experiences at the Ash Grove and the early punk rock scene had very little to do with music, but it did have to do with community. But the Ash Grove was a strange community, a strange collection of people that went to the shows that were regulars. You had every race represented, just about every economic background represented to one extent or another, although it tended to be more working class/middle class, but there was a community based around the love of this music, whether it was blues, bluegrass, or folk music. Ten years later, after the Ash Grove was gone, and that sort of community was still existing but didn't have a gathering place, you know, when I discovered the early punk rock scene, that was the first time I felt that kind of community again because rock music and pop music was no longer about clubs, it was all about basketball arenas. I never cottoned to that very well. So, suddenly, I am in these dingy clubs with oddball people from every ethnic group, every economic background, and they were all oddballs. I was like, okay, this is like being back at the Ash Grove. Maybe I'm not seeing Lightnin' Hopkins, but I can feel the sense of community. Oddly enough, the more I hung out at the scene, the more I discovered that some of the younger Ash Grove people were now part of the punk rock scene. So, it was like, OK."

And while many people may assume the Blasters were deeply focused on their record collections, or fellow travelers like Robert Gordon or Ray Campi (who was influenced by everyone from Tex Ritter and Hank Snow to the Carlisles and Maddox Brothers and Rose), punk rock and other emerging music enthralled them instead.

"If we were just focused on our record collections, I would still be at my parents' house listening to old records [*laughs*]. I would not have done anything. There was an awareness that things were going on, not particularly in the roots music department, but in the excitement, the mystery, and the confusion of the early punk rock years. We're talking about 1977–79, pre-Blasters, for us. We're all living down along Long Beach, California. We'd go up to LA and see these shows, and come back and go 'Wow,' that kind of thing. So, when we started the band, we were inspired by that energy from the scene. Technically, we were kind of hearing whatever little 45s were on Dangerhouse Records. We were listening to that. We didn't listen to Robert Gordon. We were aware of certain acts. I loved Mink DeVille. I had seen him on a tour that came through in 1978. I'm not sure if they did the whole United States, but they did a bunch of gigs in California that included Mink DeVille, Rockpile, and Elvis Costello. I went to two of those shows. This is pre-Blasters, so that kind of inspired me, like 'Gee, isn't there some way we could make music?' Because we were in our early twenties, and we kind of had given up hope. We figured our lives were over."

Other people were mining the blues as well, locally, like James Harman, who crossed paths with them.

"James had a band called the Icepick Blues Band, and James, as a guy, was kind of inspirational. He threw together the James Harman Band after the Blasters had started getting gigs up in Hollywood. But Phil and James had a band. There used to be this biker bar in West Long Beach called Sundance

James Harman Band advertisement, 1980s.

Saloon. So, James and Phil started playing at the saloon, with Bill Bateman and others. They had this combo, and they were playing there doing blues, and Phil was also doing R&B stuff, like Jackie Wilson songs. I don't know how comfortable James was with the Jackie Wilson kind of stuff because some blues guys consider R&B to be heresy. I never felt that, but some guys do. They played for two-three months there. We were always driving down to James's place and listening to old records. He would get shipments of Pearl and Lone Star beer because you couldn't get them in California in those days. It was all so exotic. We'd listen to these old blues records from the 1920s and drink through a case of beer. So, everybody was kind of influencing each other. The music we listened to mainly was what was being done in the punk rock scene. Some new wave stuff too. We all obviously loved the older music we had grown up with, and the experiences at the Ash Grove, but we were adding in this extra spice of what was happening at the moment that seemed like our passport out of a dead-end world."

Then Alvin stumbled upon Jeffrey Lee Piece.

"I had seen his name as Rankin' Jeffrey Lee in a couple of articles in *Slash*. Then in December 1979 . . . I was the "booker," the booking agent. We had a really hard time getting across the 405 Freeway, which kind of delineates, not accurately, but close enough, West/East Los Angeles. We had a hell of a time getting gigs in Hollywood and getting gigs in Santa Monica and West LA, because we didn't know anybody. Though we were going to punk rock shows, we didn't have friends. We were just guys who went to the shows. So much of the LA scene was based around friendship. If the Screamers liked X, then X would get a gig opening for Screamers, and if X liked the Dickies, the Dickies could get a gig opening for X, you know what I am saying? I don't know if any of those four bands liked each other, by the way [laughs]."

And due to luck and spontaneity, not to forget tenacity and charm, the band seized an opportunity to showcase their powerhouse stage demeanor and chops.

"We managed to get a gig playing with Levi and the Rockats in Santa Monica, and Levi and that band were great guys, but we sort of took it as a challenge. Most of our gigs involved playing biker bars for free beer, so we thought we gotta wipe the floor with these guys [Rockats]. They had all the

Next page: Levi and the Rockats, Mabuhay Gardens, San Francisco, CA. (Note: Rockats is misspelled on the flyer.)

CRIME
LEVI AND THE ROCKCATS
X-RAY TED

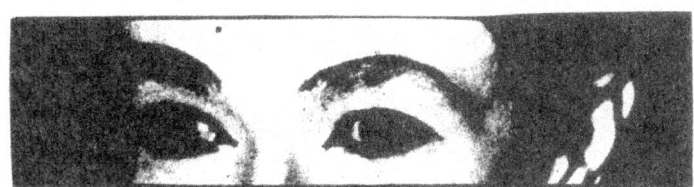

©1979 BAD DREAM IMAGE

FRIDAY MAR. 23
MABUHAY GARDENS

buzz, and they were young and cute, all the sort of things we weren't. I was only maybe two years older than Levi, but we felt older because we had experienced certain things. So, we played that gig, we really went out and blew the roof off the place. And it was really hard for them to follow us. We didn't mean to be mean, but we needed to make a statement. Because it was a little in-crowd scene, suddenly the Hollywood in-crowd saw us. This young woman at the time, Anna Statman, and her friend Pleasant Gehman, who was dating Levi, invited us, and Levi invited us too, to this party a couple of nights later at the Tropicana Hotel in West Hollywood."

And Alvin himself was the product of vital friendships that occurred during his own youth, when he too sought out music that seemed mysterious and impressive, adding to his own wealth of homegrown knowledge.

"Gene Taylor, who was the keyboard player in the Blasters, grew up with us in the Downey area. Gene was Gene when I first met him. When he was sixteen, and I was like thirteen, Gene was already the guy he is until this day. And he was already a brilliant boogie woogie blues pianist, so at a young age he got out of Downey by becoming a member of Canned Heat. I'm not sure exactly how it happened, but it happened. He was gone, out on road, living the life we all kind of wanted to live. So, through Gene, Bob Hite [of Canned Heat] entered the picture, because my brother and I had been record collectors, we were young teenagers, but we had a pretty friggin' good collection, but the great thing about Bob Hite was that he was more of an anarchist about these things. A lot of record collectors can be anal-retentive. They will let the serial number dominate over the music on the grooves. All the Victor and Columbia 78s had serial numbers on them, and some guys collected 78s based on the serial numbers. Like, 'I've got to get those numbers.' Bob Hite was the opposite of that. It was all about the music. Long before Canned Heat days, Bob had been a record collector and his pal Henry Vestine had helped in the rediscovery of Mississippi John Hurt [actually, Skip James] and people like that. So, he was all about the music and had a sort of wild anarchy passion for the music. Phil became friends with Bob. We took Jeffrey over there one night and basically blew his mind."

Understandably, one thing that still nags Alvin is that the Blasters might be discounted by historians and writers discussing the band's influence on the roots punk era.

"If you want to hear me be bitter, I'll do it for you. I don't think we get the credit we deserve for that. I'm being a Blaster now, you are not talking to Dave Alvin solo artist, you are talking to Dave Alvin from the Blasters. They are similar guys, but they are a little different. The Blasters did not get the credit for several things. One of which was, there was Mink DeVille, and the Fabulous Thunderbirds had done two albums, and there was Ray Campi, sort of, but not really. Ray was a real help to us really early in our career, but outside of England I don't know what kind of effect Ray had nationwide. Then there were others like Joe Ely, who were more geographically centered, and one or two others. In those days, outside of Mink DeVille, I hadn't become a fan of Joe Ely's yet, I like the Thunderbirds, but it was like, 'Well, that's a step in the right direction' kind of thing."

But a potent notion lingers—an insurgent roots punk style and subculture seemed to coincide, quite neatly and poignantly, with the rise of the Blasters.

"Especially on the West Coast, where a lot of our major influence was, yeah, we felt we turned on a lot of people that wouldn't normally listen to what we listened to, whether it was blues, R&B, or rockabilly. It's hard to explain, but I think a lot of American people who were fans of punk rock were looking for identities because the best punk rock, from England, was so English, as well as it should be. A lot of what the Clash were singing about in the early days was very British subject matter, so you had early American bands, and the lead singer would be singing in a British accent. Sort of like the inverse of the British invasion fifteen years earlier, when British guys were trying to sing like Ray Charles, by the late 1970s a guy from Daly City, California, might try to sing like Joe Strummer, so certain American fans of rock, new wave, and whatever else, were looking for an identity that looked more American."

And the Blasters delivered, but not without some rumbling.

"We were one of the bands that gave them, like, 'Here's an American identity for you.' I had written a song called 'American Music,' which some people took as a Reaganesque kind of tune, but the song was promoting a certain kind of American pride, which was not really going to win you a lot of fans in a certain way because we're coming out in the age of punk rock, and we're saying, 'Hey America, we're pretty cool.' It was all based on my feeling, which I had then, and I have now, which is the greatest thing about America is its music. The place where the Constitution really works is in American music. It's where the melting pot is. We had that song, and people gravitated to it, and at the time I wrote it, I hoped people would not think we were jingoistic, love-it-or-leave-it kinds of guys, because we're not. We're proud of Big Joe Turner, we're proud of Lightnin' Hopkins, and we're proud of Hank Williams. Part of our influence was giving Americans an attitude you can have: here is a look you can aspire to because we'd try to dress like the music itself. What we wore was a weird mixture of an R&B band and a honky-tonk band. Our hairstyles were as much Magic Sam and Otis Rush as they were Porter Wagoner or Billy Lee Riley. We had a look, and we had an attitude, and we didn't fuck around when we played. We played our version of roots music just louder and faster than anybody had done at that point."

But the chemistry was indelible and one-off, not something that could be duplicated or divided up into other equally potent parcels. Plus, they walked the punk line.

"If you take me out of the band, say, and you put in another guitar player and another drummer, the band would sound different. If you took out Bill Bateman and our bass player and put them in a band with James Harman and Hollywood Fats or somebody like that, they are not going to sound like the Blasters. And they don't play the way they do in the Blasters. When you get the five Blasters together, we sound like the Blasters. It's just how we play. These five guys play this way. That worked both in our favor and worked against us [laughs]. Some people were attracted to the power we could generate, and later on, when Lee Allen and Steve Berlin joined the band, the power seven guys could generate. That sort of power was the reason we could go and play with Fear or Black Flag. We could play with the Plugz, the Dickies, or the Weirdos. Yes, some punk rock kids didn't like us, but a lot did. So, it wasn't a total embrace of us, but it wasn't a total rejection. We could man-up when the time came. We could take the beer bottles and the spit, and our attitude was 'fuck you.'"

Even more importantly, perhaps, the band's open embrace of roots seemed to give permission for others to open the doors to their own heritage, like "I love punk rock, but I also love where I come from."

"So, what happened was there was a group of guys in East LA that played acoustic traditional Mexican music, and with everything that was happening in LA, they were like, 'Hey, how can we be a part of this?' They came to a Blasters gig at the Whisky A Go Go and came backstage and gave us a cassette tape of them playing electric rock 'n' roll and a little conjunto music, so we started putting them on shows opening for us, and the band was Los Lobos. I remember the first time we went to Austin, like early 1980, it was cold, and we had booked a tour of Texas and parts of the South because of our little record we had done on a rockabilly label. There was only like three, four thousand copies printed, but that record got around, so we managed to get gigs in Texas. We get to Austin, and on our first night in town, I had already seen the Dils back in the punk rock days. Now, Chip and Tony had this new band

Rank and File, Duke's, Austin, TX, 1981, by Randy "Biscuit" Tuner.

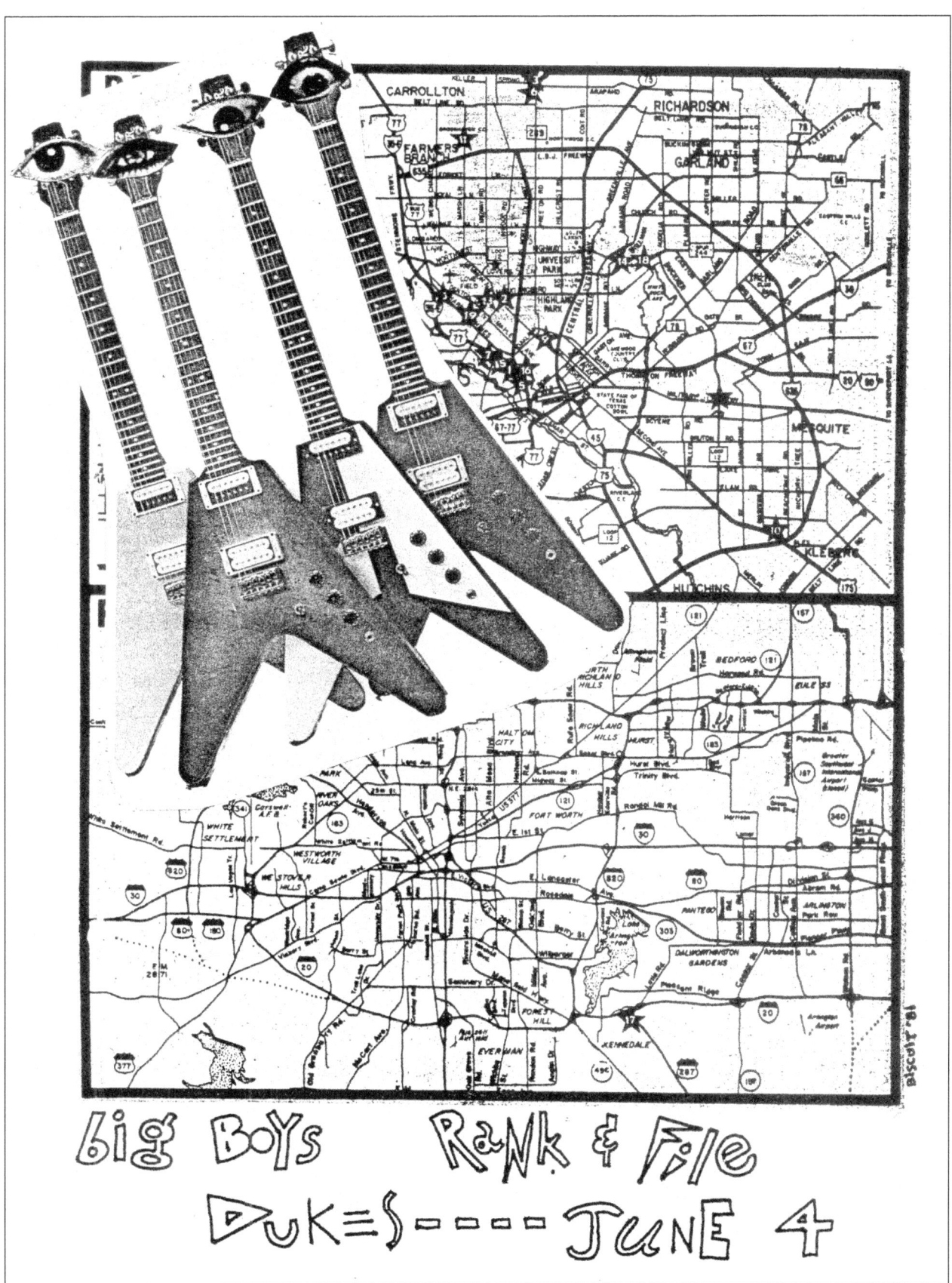

with Alejandro called Rank and File, and they were playing a gig at Club Foot opening for somebody. We went down to see them, and I was like, 'Yes! This is great!' They were still figuring out their sound, they weren't exactly there yet."

Yet, in some ways the Dils themselves had begun to mold such a tone and style at the end of their run, when their "music evoked more of the country's true greatness than any band since Creedence Clearwater Revival. In their flat, twangy vocals . . . [were] echoes of Hank Williams, Carl Perkins, and George Jones; in their slashing, slightly ragged instrumental sound, traces of every great American garage band since Elvis . . ." (Schwartz 6). To some, that may reek of hyperbole, but Rank and File definitely swam in the same currents.

By the early 1980s, the Blasters themselves seemed almost like a cornerstone, trusted by Slash to sell records and mount extensive tours, and whose opinions held sway even though a few years earlier they had gone flatly unnoticed.

"After our first album, and our live EP, Rank and File got out to LA for a couple of gigs. And in the case of both Los Lobos and Rank and File, I am going to be Blaster Dave here, with an ego, the Blasters went to Slash Records because X had told them 'You should sign the Blasters,' so we went to Slash records and said, 'Oh, you should sign Los Lobos and Rank and File. These guys are great.' We had an effect to make people like Blood on the Saddle. Even the Long Ryders and people like that realized that it was okay to be yourself, it was okay to love the Clash and the Jam but you could also love Muddy Waters and Conway Twitty [laughs]. You didn't want to define yourself in opposition to whatever was happening in England, but you could be yourself. To me, punk rock was always about, at least in the early days, expanding, being the oddball you are, not the oddball you are supposed to be, which is what it became later on. It happened with hippies, it happened with beatniks, it happened with beboppers. When anything becomes codified—okay, this is what we are now, and we are nothing else but this—then those scenes kind of die or wither on the vine. If you look at what Slash put out, it's a pretty wide range of sounds. It did have a band like Fear, but you also had Green on Red. Yes, they sort of put out a Flesh Eaters record, and then you had Rank and File."

However, after only a few years upon busting through the cracks of LA punk and solidifying an alternative to the cropped-hair, charred chords, speed-choked (both in terms of pills and tempos) masses, the era was already showing its decline.

"The end of the era was like the end of the Roman empire. The end wasn't a solid date. It was fuzzy. In a way, things started to change in 1982, to be safe. Things started to change for the whole scene when the Go-Go's hit it really big. They had always been a great band and a different vibe in the early days, but when they hit it big, they had decided to go full-on less punk rock and more pop rock. They hit it huge, the cover of *Rolling Stone*, the whole bit, multiple hit singles off the album. That sort of led . . . There had always been around that scene a little bit of jealousy and competition, but it had always been the positive kind of competition, like 'Hey, did you hear the Plimsouls' new song? Hey, did you hear that new X thing? Did you hear what the Blasters did?' Then people would say, 'Yeah, I want to do something like that too. I can do that but better or different.' There was that kind of positive notion back and forth between artists."

But money charged in, at first unwanted and even recognized by many acts as something to reject and despise, but as soon as it did appear, it changed the dynamics and psychology, the desires and the tensions.

"But then the Go-Go's hit it big, it was like, 'Fuck, the Go-Go's are huge!' They are going around with tour buses and playing big-ass shows. The women themselves didn't change that much in general. We did a lot of gigs opening for them after they hit it big. So, but what happened was the idea of limousines starting [taking hold] and the whole thing of, 'Why them and not us?' You have to remember, I am going to sound like an old man here, most of those bands that are now considered classic bands, could not get a record deal or get on the radio, if they had a record deal. Because of the production value of the Go-Go's, the old school girl group production slid them right onto the radio. X, partially because of the sound of their records sounded squashed compared to the sonics of what was on normal or standard FM radio those days, did not get a lot of airplay. And the Plimsouls didn't get a lot of airplay until 'A Million Miles Away,' even though they had done their major label record and had gone nowhere because they couldn't get people to play it."

But the scene was now forever changed, sometimes by the rise of new bands, sometimes by the raw, ugly underbelly of destructive urges.

"So, when they were off their major label, they made their greatest record ever, which got them back on a major label. You could start to see things gray a little. The other reason was, in the early days, nobody was touring, or if they toured it was for a week, 'Hey we got gigs in Seattle, Vancouver, and Portland.' And we'd be like, 'Be careful out there,' but then people were touring for two-three months. Before that, everybody saw each other almost every day. People were hanging out, whether at the Starwood, Whiskey, Hong Kong Café, whatever club. People were always around, talking about whatever band they saw or a good place to get beer after 2 a.m. When everybody started getting record deals, whether major labels or independents, whether Slash or Columbia, people started touring. In the case of the Blasters, we would be gone a month or two months sometimes. We would go to Europe and be based out of London. Then you came home, and it took you a week to get readjusted to the scene because it had changed. And some of the changes were great. Like one time I came back after three months and suddenly there was groups like the Long Ryders were starting up or Salvation Army or Dream Syndicate. I was like, 'Whoa, this is different than everything I saw right before I left town.'"

"By 1986, there was still enough of a scene around to still feel like the scene, but by 1987–88, it was gone. Back then I used the analogy of, someone had a fire underneath the coffee pot, and they never took it off the stove, so what happened is that all you had left was these burnt grounds. There was more and more heroin: less and less brilliance, and more stupidity. So, with the brilliant bands, they were on tour, or the people had drifted into other types of music, whether world music or western swing. They weren't interested that much in punk rock, or anything else like that. In the past, if drugs were involved, they were involved in a goofball way. In the early days, it was all about the music and about the bands, the energy; so five years later, people were more concerned about so-so getting a bunch of heroin. It wasn't about their music, it was about the drugs and alcohol or the social scene, more gossipy."

Though Alvin grew well beyond that scene and into a long arc of a solo career spanning decades, he has also remained quintessentially himself, a roots punk at heart, and not watered down or mutated beyond recognition by trends and corporate music pressures.

"I'm basically a thrasher," Alvin intones. "But if Lightnin' Hopkins was a thrasher, then that's how I play guitar. The great thing about blues, and one of the reasons it has survived, is that it's not a monolithic thing, though some people try to make it fit into a monolithic identity. It's everything from a shuffle band playing Antone's on a Monday night to Miles Davis and Jimmie Rodgers. The form itself is a poetic form like haiku or a sonnet. It all depends on what you do with that form. You can have a Shakespearian sonnet or a modern sonnet. In the hands of the right person, a sonnet can be a sonnet without seeming like it. Aram Saroyan did a whole book on twelve bizarre sonnets,

The Blasters, Hong Kong Café, Los Angeles, CA.

but they were all in classical sonnet form, though you wouldn't recognize it. It's just a form. There're so many types of blues, there's Texas blues, Delta blues, Chicago blues, Memphis, Chicago, St. Louis, and they're all different. I tend to be more aggressive when I play guitar, which comes from the punk stuff, and because I'm not one of the world's greatest guitarists, so I just turn up the volume louder so no one will notice [*laughs*]."

3

ELVIS VS. EL VEZ

Johnny [Rotten] was embarrassing onstage, he wasn't as wild as before. I'm fed up. It's better to quit this way than to end up like Elvis . . .

—Sid Vicious, *Hit Parader*, 1978

"Elvis was a hero to most / but he didn't mean shit to me," rapped Public Enemy on "Fight the Power," with obvious disdain, as they launched their pithy, pointed salvo against the pop culture figure beloved by millions. Yet, on a much smaller scale, and rather disarming in a nonchalant way, my own mother told me, even as she knew my aunt collected Elvis singles galore, that "I wouldn't even cross the street to see him." Most noticeably, this was true because she admired Gene Vincent instead, a singer of inveterate cool eulogized in an Ian Dury tune with lyrics such as "Let the blue roll tonight / At the sock hop ball in the union hall / Where the bop is their delight."

So, while Vincent caused swoons and provided a fashion template for Billy Idol, who sought to emulate his leather jacket chic (Idol 96), Elvis now seems to cause a partisan brawl amid music lovers. Some insisted, with ongoing invectives, that he was no more than a common thief that exploited Black music; others simply cast him as bubblegum, while others imagine a figure that might be a punk precursor: bold and incantatory. Yet, as Barry Henssler of Necros/Big Chief noted, "They sell danger and you buy danger. It's age old. Rebellion has been marketed . . . since Elvis Presley" (Buj). That teen spirit might feel manufactured, even though initially "Presley shook up the world," argues writer Jon Young in a profile of bands like Gang of Four, "with a vengeance, angering and frightening an unprepared Establishment" (29).

"Elvis was to me the same as Jimmy Swaggart, or Patti Smith, the same as James Brown," avows M. Gira, singer of Swans. "They're just perfectly tuned conduits for the massively powerful life-creating/destroying energy that exists inside us and around us, and they managed to find a form that it could inhabit

El Vez, 100 Club, London, UK, by Graham Russell.

and use as a voice. A very, very few times, I've been able to occupy that privileged position too, but not often, and I don't feel any personal responsibility for it or even feel that I had much to do with it, except for maybe arranging the circumstance that made it possible to exist; then, since I'm there, it comes through me. I've been thinking about this a lot lately: who writes my songs? As I said, I don't think I do it. So, naturally, I just wrote a song about the subject, but again, I don't think I wrote it. It's a prayer, sort of, to the 'entity' that writes the songs. It's like a hymn. The chorus is 'may freedom and love, come through to you, through this song.' Corny, I guess, but it seems right."

Though that mystique remains palpable for some, Elvis-as-punk is still hotly debated. "Sure, Elvis made an impact," argues Chip Kinman, guitarist and

46 Elvis vs. El Vez

singer for the Dils. "But Elvis was by no means a punk. There were no punks until there were punks." The logic for him is a closed circle. Punks begat punk.

"My parents didn't leave the Middle East. They were thrown out. Everything my daddy had was nationalized," tells Sylvain Sylvain, guitarist for the New York Dolls. "But then again, it was in the middle of the whole Zionist thing, so being a Jew in Egypt in the middle of the 1950s was not the smartest thing I guess, although we had been there for centuries and centuries, but anyway it definitely did . . . I still use that tabla thing, the Arabic thing. That's still in my rock 'n' roll. And when we moved to France, all the kids in Paris . . . well, my brother took me to see *King Creole* by Elvis Presley in the movie houses over there. The only way I can describe it to you is like going to see that scary one over here [*Rocky Horror Picture Show*] when everyone comes in and sings along all dressed up. It was just like that. All the guys had the haircut, the pompadour haircuts like Elvis, and they all brought guitars and bongos, and the girls were dancing in the aisles. I said, 'Oh my god.' I loved it. There were all kinds of rock 'n' roll stars that were on the radio at the time in Paris when I was growing up. It introduced me to rock 'n' roll, and I didn't know it was American rock 'n' roll. I thought it was French, like Johnny Hallyday singing [Sylvain sings first in French, then in English], "It's my party and I'll cry if I want to." Eddie Cochran was amazing, like huge in France, but Johnny was bigger than Eddie Cochran. I got introduced to all that stuff. It was amazing. So, when I got to the states, I was already all into it."

Still, though Cochran and Hallyday were mavericks, as roots-rocker Mojo Nixon raucously yawped, "Elvis Is Everywhere!" And in the spectrum of American indie and punk music, that seems truer than ever: band names abound in both dark and pedestrian tribute (Velvet Elvis, Elvis Hitler, Helvis, Elvis Brothers), advertising campaigns included headlines like "Dead Elvis Back" published by Toxic Shock Records, bands like Adrenalin OD graced their album titles with his persona (*Cruising with Elvis in Bigfoot's UFO*) or bands like Big Boys had posthumous anthologies named *Skinny Elvis* and *Fat Elvis.* X mentions a homeless man ranting about Elvis in their tune "Back 2 the Base," while the Butthole Surfers conjure a bastardized monster of him on "The Revenge of Anus Presley." Active Ingredients featured a T-shirt design, "Visit Elvis in Hell," that somehow flew beneath the copyright laws, while Target Video's "After Hours" featured Elvis getting his hair buzzed off, with a target situated on his forehead and the text "I Ran, I Rock, I Roll" boldly projected across the top. *Southern Healer* fanzine ran an ad in Flipside that read, in hand-scrawled letters: "Memphis Killed Elvis." Meanwhile, Th'Inbred totally swiped *Kissin' Cousins* for an album title, plus repurposed the Elvis movie poster for their advertising, while the album cover for *London Calling*, by the Clash, is a direct nod to Elvis Presley's debut album art and design.

Elvis lyrical fodder included SNFU's "Head Smashed in a Buffalo Jump" ("He looked a lot like Elvis / long before his name became disgraced"), the Dead Kennedys' "Kidnap" ("Kidnap John Wayne & Debbie Boone / Let's invade Elvis Presley's tomb"), as well as "For the Love of Ivy" by the Gun Club ("You look just like an Elvis from hell"). Alan Vega, singer for synth-punk pioneers Suicide, had previously obsessed over mid-century doo-wop and experimental jazz and had an eerily soulful voice described as a "fine mutant Elvis" (Young 44), which might be a phrase more apt for Nick Cave's harrowing, atavistic "Tupelo": from 1985, the atmospheric tune that begins with claps of thunder and downpouring sheets of rain, is a brooding, dark-dreamy, percussive, and groaning soar-throat ode to the city that gave rise to the King.

"I have no interest in being an Elvis Presley clone or anything like that," Cave intoned to *Sounds* in 1985. "'Tupelo' is really an old blues song by John Lee Hooker called 'Tupelo Blues' . . . It's about a storm that brought a big flood down on Tupelo, only I haven't used those lyrics. I've written my own to introduce the concept of Elvis being born there, and to give it an Old Testament feel" (14).

Punk bands offered an endless series of covers, including the likes of Hickoids delivering a scorching lounge-punk inferno of "Burnin' Love" and Dead Kennedys swung with a San Francisco aberration of "Viva Las Vegas." Leatherface, including raspy-voiced singer Frankie Stubbs, crooned "Can't Help Falling in Love With You" and forcibly belted out "In the Ghetto." Then, in a bareboned and lighter solo outing, a contrast to the densely guitar-strewn band version, he again unveiled "I Can't Help . . ." and penned "Old Elvis." In fact, a writer for *The Guardian* described Stubbs's distinct, wizened warble as "a bit like Lemmy [of Motorhead] singing the blues or Elvis gargling gravel" (McMahon).

Elvis often serves as a milestone and counterweight to the gamut of music that rang false to some punks. As Vic Bondi of Articles of Faith intoned to me, "For every Elvis, Ramones and Clash, there's a Night Ranger, Britney Spears, or Lady Gaga."

As Walt Whitman once wrote about himself, perhaps Elvis contained multitudes and can be a considered a multiverse; someone referenced on *London Calling* album art and design by the Clash, inspiring club names like the Velvet Elvis, a club in Houston sued by the Elvis estate for copyright

Elvis Hitler, The Axiom, Houston, TX.

Nick Knox, the Cramps, by Edward Colver.

infringement, and part of the visual vernacular at Alex's Bar in Long Beach, which features velvet portraits of him while Mike Watt, Manic Hispanic, and the Adolescents sizzle on stage.

As Lux Interior of the Cramps explained to MTV on the twentieth anniversary of the performer's death, "Whence Elvis sprang it all," while Poison Ivy noted, "It's like he's in our blood" (qtd. in Nelson). They were "Elvis-o-philes," collecting almost each of his original singles and showcasing items relating to him on their *A Date with Elvis* album cover. To them and others, Elvis was a huge portion of the Rosetta Stone, shaped by Black R&B and jumpy, twitchy country as well, that unlocked rock 'n' roll libido, physicality, and musical possibilities beyond teen cults.

"The Cramps are rockabilly punk," explains Peter Case. "Ivy and Lux were huge record collectors, but they were on the rockabilly tip, not the blues tip. For me, just a band going to Memphis is not enough to make them real honest, real, and sincere. Anybody can go to Memphis and try to cop some

Elvis vs. El Vez

vibes. What made them feel real to me was when I went to the Troubadour and saw them play live. They just blew me away, man. I taped that show on a cassette player. It was probably my top-played tape in the 1980s. It was a bit rough, but it was so fucking great. They were extraordinary. They were like the Ramones of roots-rock. They were a huge influence on what the Gun Club sounded like, what they allowed themselves to do, and to the flamboyance of what Jeffrey put on as the leader of the band. Jeffrey had this incredible kind of showmanship, and so did Lux, not to forget Ivy. I guess in some sense they are novelty, but there was something so rockin' about what they did. At that point, to be committed to playing novelty songs, like that, was like a huge statement."

"When I saw the Cramps in 1979, the room was packed with all different kinds of people, not just a room full of punk rockers," Ian MacKaye of Fugazi and Minor Threat recalls, "though there were punk rockers there of all shapes and sizes. Bad Brains were there handing out flyers for their first show. There were junkie-type people, a huge political contingent, and these crazy redneck hillbilly punker-type kids. It was the first time since the radical 1960s-type stuff that I had seen people like this. And I said, here it is. This is what I'm looking for. It was the people who were on the margins of society, and that's where I always felt I belonged. There were people challenging political conventions, musical conventions, artistic conventions, sexual conventions, and psychological conventions. People were testing every water there was to be had. It was all there, and the show was a cathartic experience."

"I saw the Cramps in the winter of 1978," recalls Robert Lopez (El Vez), "and that was roots rock at its finest because there was a whole vein of Hasil Adkins and that kind of stuff that the Cramps were mining. There was the rockabilly idea but even darker—like Delta blues is scarier than regular blues. They were scarier, darker-tinged. At that point, it was weird, because I was going away from punk as the clubs were closing more, and it was starting to be taken over by the Orange County scene, and it was becoming more hardcore. Before, punk was originally full of variations. I mean, people who dressed up, people who dressed down, boys, girls, people of color, music that was jazzy, music that was angular, music that was Ramones-like. Suddenly, it became we all wear the same jeans and shirts and the fast hardcore style became the mainstream of what punk rock represented. I went to other things in 1979. That was when I was in Catholic Discipline, who was already a post-punk idea of 'Let's use other influences' because it was becoming more mainstream, as in hardcore is what sells to the jocks and to the high school kids of Orange

The Cramps, by Tim O'Brien.

Previous page: The Cramps and Nick Cave, Perkins Palace, Pasadena, CA.

County and the white suburban guys. That was not as appealing as it used to be. Let's go into these other ideas and style and influences."

That rock 'n' roots energy, both a Cramps and early Elvis signature, is a thread that stitches them together, however uneasily, for it defines the sheer audacity of their efforts, their incalculable cool, their brazen and bewitching brew, as well as their ability to push a seismic change in music and culture. In fact, as Lux intoned to *Chic* magazine, "We may revive aspects . . . but I think we're more of a modernist band . . . If we're revivalists, we're reviving the rockabilly stance. And that's something that should be revived. There's too much humility slopping up the world these days" ("The Cramps: Voodoo" 18).

Or, as James Stevenson, guitarist for Gen X, the Alarm, and Gene Loves Jezebel argues, "There has always been music that challenges the status quo—right back to Robert Johnson and the original blues guys, and then Woody Guthrie, etc., and then rock and roll. Even Elvis, well in some ways especially Elvis, made people question their beliefs and changed opinion by causing a conflict between the young and what the older generation held as sacred. I think punk still does that—though we're not all so young anymore!"

The impact of Elvis on punk seems confusing and contradictory, something that needs to continuously be addressed, grasped, and discerned. Music mattered, looks mattered, attitude mattered.

Elvis vs. El Vez

The Cramps, Hammersmith Palais, London, UK, 1981 newspaper advert.

"I was a medium-huge Elvis fan. It was more about the shtick of it," explains Dave Dictor of MDC. "In the late 1980s, hardcore was falling apart, and everyone was doing something really crazy and different. One tour I went out as Divine after Divine died. It was the Mourn Divine Correctly tour. We didn't do an album but hooked up with some of the people from the Popstitutes. That was one entity. And then I started doing Elvis."

In some ways, Dictor's sudden mutation into a punk Elvis was entirely happenstance. "One day I was hanging out with Rebecca Sevrin of Frightwig, and she was a seamstress who said, 'Let me make an outfit for you,' and someone said make it like Elvis. I don't think I even asked for it myself. There was a Halloween thing coming up, so she made me this great Elvis outfit. I didn't take it off for a year. I was walking around with a girdle sticking out of the top of it with my hairy chest. There was this great sexcore thing going on in San Francisco at the time with bands like Tragic Mulatto, some funny people. They had people on stage squirting hot dogs out of their assholes. It was a very eclectic scene and on the edge. I could see that hardcore was dying down: DRI was going, but RKL had some deaths in the band . . . that is what slowed them down and then finished them as a band, and Toxic Reasons broke up. You could go up and down the list of all the great bands. Minor Threat, SS Decontrol, Black Flag, all gone. Agnostic Front kept going, and they had that East Coast thing, but the West Coast was different. The bands that were big in 1986 were gone by 1990."

The Elvis shtick upended the macho clone norms of punk, rooted MDC's music in a hammy and beloved side of the past and seemed to spark a rejuvenation of sorts too. Dictor, by the end, had become an ambassador and interpreter of American music.

Swine King, Emo's, Austin, TX, by Randy "Biscuit" Turner, 1993.

"So, I started to wear the Elvis outfit and went on tour, and I stayed in Europe and walked around Berlin playing acoustic guitar. Of course, I am going to play 'Love You Tender' and sing all those tunes. Then I came back to the U.S., and people would yell at me, 'Blue Suede Shoes'! And we started doing it. I always felt connected to rock 'n' roll. We used to do 'Toffuti,' our take on Little Richard, and we used to do 'Jailhouse Rock' as 'Dead Cops Rock.' We'd slip into all kinds of personas. We just had that weird sense of humor. Of course, there were always these 'Class of 1988' punk rock kids who didn't want something different. But I just couldn't do 'I am Dave Dictor, put the 8-track in the machine and let me spit it out for you.'"

Plus, the Elvis and Divine personas also had the added appeal of allowing the sexual spectrum to be explored.

Elvis vs. El Vez

MDC, Elvis in the Rhineland advert, *Maximum Rocknroll*, 1988.

"I would come out as Elvis and blow people's heads. And when I did it as Divine, it really blew people's head because people would see that whole trans rock 'n' roll energy. But I was living in San Francisco, where they had homocore, a big gay scene. I knew the Tribe 8 people. There were all kinds of cool people, like Pansy Division. We played with them all. I wasn't the totally gay person, but the 'kind-of' gay person. I had the reputation of being the gayest straight person anyone knew. I would say, 'I am not straight, you are just seeing me wrong. I am trans everything. I'm genderfuck. I relate to everyone and everybody.' There's a piece of me in everything. And I want to represent everybody, so yes, I am part Divine, part Elvis, and part hardcore, part punk rock, and I'm Otis Redding. I am everything. Because that's everything that created me. That's my story, and I am sticking to it."

On one hand, the King's influence seems almost immense and Herculean, as if he set off a tidal wave of possibilities regarding psycho-sexual marauding; musical aberration and hybridity, retreat and reinvention; endless camp and schmaltz; brouhaha and brooding; money and vision. On the other hand, he seems a quirk in the trajectory of punk, an indulgence with a wink, and a masquerade of masks. To that end, he inspired an entire alias and persona—El Vez, the ongoing project of Robert Lopez, one of the most intriguing figures in punk history. With roots in bands such as the Zeros and Catholic Discipline, by the 1990s he spun a new identity that mixed class consciousness, identity politics, Hispanic pride, and pop culture appropriation and disruption. Part performance artist, part rebel rouser, part wooning singer, his panache and irony, plus limitless gusto and charm, are rarely matched.

"In 1977, Elvis is not at his best," Lopez argues. "We are young, we are sixteen. What are we against? We are against stuff like that! Man, look at how over-bloated he has become. It's the campness. As a young, sixteen-year-old punk, it was about who was with us and who's against us. Elvis is what we were trying not to be. It was like, 'We are new. We do not need to use old icons to represent what we are expressing.' Although then you get older and you realize, oh, it's all the same roots because he was the punk rock of 1955. He was the starting of something new—the playing of something traditional, as in country, but doing it faster, just as we were doing stuff that was faster. I don't have any real pivotal moment with his music. In El Vez, it was like a shorter point of reference, like I will use this image because you understand that should be in your musical knowledge, so I am using this as a point of reference to recall these other images and other ideas and then flipping it with a moustache, etc."

Of course, Lopez was also cognizant of a roots music emergence that was gaining steam and attention.

"Los Lobos were playing a little bit then, since they had been around since that period, but they hadn't done 'La Bamba' and all that. *How Will the Wolf Survive* hadn't even come out. But at sixteen, I can remember thinking, 'That's too beaner for me.' Meaning, why would you want to do that? I am not my parents. I am not my uncles. I am a defiant sixteen-year-old. I mean, punk rock is perfect for a sixteen-year-old because it is like discovering what you can get away with, what are the boundaries, what is acceptable and what's not, but I think one of the points was: that's my past, that's my family. I am a teenager of 1976. We got the Ramones. We got the Sex Pistols. We don't need to use these traditions. Of course, now as we get older, you say, that's why I like this, because that's the kind of stuff my parents and uncles played. That's where I learned these guitar bits. But I recall thinking as a teen that I don't want to be like that."

Yet, despite being a modern "year zero" youth seemingly shorn of the past, ready to rock to his own beat, he was entirely the product of deep ethnic awareness.

"I grew up with Chicano culture because my aunts and uncles worked at Plaza De La Raza in San Diego, so we were aware of the art of Cinco De Mayo, Frida Kahlo, Diego Rivera, etc. We knew different folklorico dances, we knew food traditions, Aztecs and Mayans, etc., that kind of stuff. I always assumed that every culture had their own—you have a Ukrainian dancehall, you have been taught the ways of your people because I knew America was a melting pot filled with people from all different places.

"So, I assumed that everyone was schooled in their heritage, which later I found out that people aren't. That's partly due to the frivolity and stupidity of youth to think, okay, I am something new, this hasn't been done before. Later, you realize it has roots in the Beats, or roots in the Dadaists, all that stuff. But at the time, it's like, we're the first hippies ever. We're Beats, people interested in poetry! But all the styles come from older ones, but the nice thing about being an actual punk rocker at sixteen, as opposed to everyone else, who was at least a good five, ten years older than us, they were still twenty-five, twenty-six, we were sixteen, is we were actual teenagers writing actual teenage lyrics, as opposed to a twenty-six-year-old thinking, let me ape the style of a mad angry kid! Like, the *Sniffin' Glue* version of that!"

Plus, because his past was so self-evident, he felt more freedom to explore and redefine himself.

"Being secure in my own culture, I was free to reject it, does that make sense? I was schooled enough and confident enough to reject it and say, I am modern youth. Of course, later you understand it stems from what you knew, how you grew up, and why you like certain things. In my later years, I went back and collected all that. So, that was the nice thing. It didn't matter much then, in terms of being Latino, because we were all misfits. You could be gay, straight, a woman, of color, and we were all weirdoes before people were even yelling Devo because Devo came out later. Most of us had come from glitter rock roots, but the 'now' was punk rock. It was small enough that we couldn't say, no Latinos allowed, or we Latinos are going to subsect."

"Later, it became, we are hardcore, no girls allowed or people of color, when it became larger and more marketable. There was enough audience that we could separate ourselves. Before that, it was, we are all the misfits. And if you look at any old footage, there are people with long hair. We weren't yelling, you get out of here, cause you are a hippie! It was a mix of people. It wasn't just the modern kids all wearing trash bags, it was a mix people still in flares, people with long hair: it was all are welcome, and it was a mix of gays and women. And, those mix of gays and straights would be on stage also, yet later it turned into this white male thing."

So, hardcore became that dividing line between eras, people, and scenes.

"In punk, we didn't think we're Latinos, let's huddle together, it was something you didn't have to do. We were all uniform in our misfit-ideology. We were all freaks at school. We were all outsiders, and so here were the outsiders, and we knew there was a bunch of them in England and we knew there was a bunch of them in New York, and we were the bunch in LA. We, as the Zeros, would get a weekend of that, then have to go back to school in San Diego. So, we were even more estranged or had to ponder what we had seen, what styles, what music, etc., then go home to the real world as opposed to those who could have that five nights a week, if they cared to."

His El Vez albums like *G.I. Ay, Ay! Blues* critique and evoke a whole array of issues. Those include the "inevitable commercialization of ethnic subcultures" awash in lines from "Si I am a Lowrider" (a re-worked version of "C.C. Rider") that delves into an entire nation of rappers and "lowriders on MTV," as El Vez sings (Priewe 277). Hence, El Vez is deploying both subversive (to draw attention to limitless corporate grabs of subculture style) and self-reflexive (to draw attention to his own people and culture) ruptures of content, style, and meaning. In effect, El Vez supplements the apolitical Elvis tunes with an injection of resistance inside the kernel of performances by Elvis that were themselves already culturally pertinent and eruptive. El Vez grafts his politics onto the form (273).

"Well, it's the Statue of Liberty, 'bring me your homeless, your tired and wear' melting pot kind of idea," Lopez reveals. "What is America? Is it apple pie? It can be tamale pie too. The idea is that America is sauerkraut, America is sopapillas, America is chop suey, America is all these different things because America is based on the idea of immigration and people from other lands coming to this land to mix it all up together and establish themselves with other cultures, so to be of a different culture is an American thing. The whole thing of Elvis as an icon is pretty American, and I superimpose on it and put a moustache on it, but it could be easily become a Black one, or a pan-Asian idea of what it could be. Like taking those cultural ideas and applying this American pie Elvis and saying, this is what America is about too."

Lopez continues: "Things can be questioned, analyzed, and changed or stay the same. You can look at things many different ways. When I had different shows, like the Gospel Show, or the Rock and Revolution, or El Vez for Prez, I'm not really running for president or trying to be a spiritual leader. I don't have a political manifesto, but I'm trying to open the door for debate or trying to get you to think about it or say here's a possibility. I'm not saying this is the end-all, be-all, and this is the way you should see God. Or this is the end-all, be-all, the correct political way things should go. I just want people to think. I want people to laugh, because when you are smiling or laughing you are more open to different views and ideas. The idea of taking something you know, like Elvis, and saying, how about looking at things this way, it's like turning it upside down and putting a moustache on it. It's still that Elvis idea, but here's a new point of view of it."

"Robert is an absolutely brilliant guy," argues bass player David Jones, "He is a master at taking these well-known songs and transforming the lyrics into political, satirical, and poignant anthems with his own themes... it was a blast to play 'Aztlan' [a critique of the hypocrisy of US/Mexico border policy by Robert Lopez, set to the music of "Graceland" by Paul Simon], "Chicanisma," about Chicana empowerment set to Elvis Presley's "Little Sister," and "En El Barrio," a Chicano slice-of-life portrait set to Elvis Presley's "In the Ghetto." Jones, who has also played with Deadbeats, Alice Bag, and others, stresses, "He manages to put together a thoroughly entertaining visual and musical show while delivering a powerful social and political message."

"I am not an impersonator," Lopez confided to me. "... I'm more like a translator, so it's not like a full-on impersonation of Elvis. Names are just a way of helping you get a grip on something, but when you see the show, or listen to it, people say, this is completely not what I thought it would be like. I don't mind labels because I always think I break them. So, it doesn't bother me."

But El Vez is not entirely singular in his approach or style, as the singer and guitarist of La Tuya reminded me. As a music journalist for *Razorcake* and other publications over the years and an ardent chronicler of punk history, Jimmy Alvarado has painstakingly detailed the unique punk scene of East LA that is dominated by Latinos. As he reveals, "I thought El Vez's shtick was funny, but, again—and not to take anything away from his efforts, 'cause he's brilliant in his own right—he's pulling from a long history of Raza commenting/parodying pop culture, like Lalo Guerrero's English version of 'Elvis Perez' recorded in the 1970s with a couple of the dudes from Los Lobos, if I am not mistaken. It's a parody he originally wrote and recorded in Spanish in the 1950s. In all honesty, Don Lalo," who began in Los Angeles with the quartet Los Carlistas, "is probably one of the most criminally overlooked American musicians this country has produced. He's originally from Tucson, Arizona," where he was steeped in both American pop culture and the traditional music and culture of the Mexican American community there.

"He wrote his first song, 'Cancion Mexicana,' when he was a teenager, a song which is now considered the unofficial mariachi anthem. He was one of the pioneers of pachuco swing. In fact, his tunes comprise the bulk of the tunes in the movie/play *Zoot Suit*. Plus, he wrote many other standards in the

Mexican canon, mambos, boleros, corridos, crooner-type tunes in English, crazy rock/ranchera hybrids, and had a popular set of children's albums, sort of the Spanish version of the Chipmunks. He also wrote a lot of parodies in both English and Spanish and continued to play and record until he passed away in 2005 at the age of eighty-eight."

Hence, just as El Vez is dynamic, ever-inventive, and in pursuit of a wild ensemble of styles and high energy, Guerrero was a precursor, adding flair like mambo and rumba, plus mariachi and rock hybridity; Guerrero employed "linguistic code-switching" and layered songs with social commentary, like addressing the Chicano movement, United Farm Workers, and other activist issues (Chable 597). But his undertow of humor in many tunes made him ear-friendly, though he did encounter some bumps along the way. That included his tune "The Ballad of Pancho López," a reimagined riff on "Davy Crockett," which traded on negative stereotypes and was subsequently tossed off set lists by Guerrero himself, who eventually received National Folk Treasure status proffered by the Smithsonian Institution (597–98).

Hence, Robert Lopez and Lalo Guerrero are of different generations but are knitted together: Guerrero as a kind of precursor, paving a path, Lopez bringing his authentic punk bravado and ingredients to the mix, and each embodying an utter sense of promise and commitment to entertainment laced with conscience.

Or as Lopez himself told me: "When you are young, you are moving on the energy of youth, and as you develop more ideas, you have more things you want to say in certain ways. I think that getting the agenda out is more my call now with El Vez. Just to get issues across or keep people more aware, especially in these times when things are in a conservative cycle back again. Ideas like border issues and other things are swept under the table unless you are the thorn in the side, or the thorn underneath the rose, or whatever you want to be. You have to be the agitator and bring it up again. I choose to verbalize it in songs."

And like Guerrero, El Vez, too, has wrestled with the consequence of employing stereotypes: "I mean, El Vez is an extreme of how Mexican I can be. It's overblown, and it's also an idea of an Elvis. No one really takes an Elvis impersonator very seriously. They're almost American court jesters. The idea of making it a Mexican one with charro, style, and flash is to gild that lily even more. But to have words of truth—revolution, safe sex, and Latino heroes—coming through that messenger is to completely confuse the issue and enhance the issues at the same time. I think there are stereotypes of every culture, and I think that's fine. When I see the Chihuahua commercial for Taco Bell or Speedy Gonzalez, I don't think that's how people view me. Because sure there's Mexicans with accents, and sure there might be lazy Mexicans, but there's lazy white people, there's lazy Black people, there's lazy everybody. There's fast-talking Mexicans, there's fast-talking Japanese, there's fast-talking Black people. Every culture can be stereotyped, but it does not mean that every person is that way. I, for one, don't think that way, and think it includes all the people. Stereotypes can be used for humor sometimes, and I super blow them up, and then empower them with knowledge, strength, and issues that can be addressed."

That Guerrero also agitated by using folk idioms, rock 'n' roll, and Latino cultural influences as his engines makes El Vez no less special: it makes the work webbed and intertextual, like a conversation between eras and epochs.

Certainly, that does not make it less "authentic," pertinent, or potent. Lopez continues: "Authenticity, whether being in painting, being in cooking, being in music, well, all good stuff is a collage in reference to other points. I mean, John and Paul [the Beatles] were referencing something else. Cooking is, I need this, but I didn't have any cilantro, so I used this instead. It's all a mix, and people get too hung up on authenticity, and maybe I don't because it's part of the camp or part of the political, or part of the funny, or part of the rocking, is that you are mixing: I am referencing glam and I am dressed as an Aztec god, now I am referencing Elvis; so I don't worry about authenticity because I just crossed three lines of time, culture, and musical references, from Aztec culture to Elvis's southern culture, so I don't think about that. But they are all things that have inspired me. Those are things that authentically inspired me, but I am not going to worry about saying, is the traditional way that the glam rockers of 1972 wore their heels because I can't go to those stores anymore, so I made them myself. Is that authentic, making it yourself? Is that as authentic as buying the real platform shoe that was worn? I do not have a mellotron, like they had 'Strawberry Fields Forever,' so I took this harmonica and did it. Is that not authentic? The authentic one is the mellotron on key 32, but I don't have that, and part of that is economy, part of it is what you have references to, and not all Latinos are not rich and have access to all that, so you make it yourself, you bend it."

Hence, the people who define terms like authenticity, which is itself a moving target, are often themselves people of privilege, status, power, and resources.

"Oh, it's not authentic western wear: I used a Sharpie and some pins. Authenticity, although I can admire it, changes with culture, which keeps on moving, and all people don't have access to all instruments, materials, fabrics, money, etc., to do what the authentic might be. It changes left and right. One of the things I would really like to see is go to Dubai because a lot of the workers there come from the Philippines, India, Turkey, etc. And there is this mythos that, because all the rich people work at the hotels, etc., that these people in the ghetto were taken out of their elements and were thrown into the desert, so they are like, 'You listen to that kind of music?' Or, 'I don't have the papaya like you get in Mexico, but I have found this weird fruit,' so you end up with mixed music and food. Then it's so hot, I can't wear my usual, so look, I made this out of that. And that is culture moving because you make things with what you have, and who's to say that is not authentic? Are you saying my culture ends because I am not in the Philippines? It keeps on moving forward, changing. Culture is a living thing. Certainly, there are points where you can say, 'They did it like this.' And that's a point. That's not the end-all, be-all. My notion of authenticity is like, as my grandmother would say, 'Cinnamon? We don't have cinnamon here. We use nutmeg.' Is that less authentic? The same thing goes for music and art, clothes and costumes."

4

GARY FLOYD

Heart and Mind with the Power of a Freight Train

Gary Floyd is an underground gay and punk music legend, almost bar none. For years, he seemed like a music-based preacher entangled in fiery outrage, venomous lyrics, outlaw sexuality, and barbed left-wing politics. The Texas-based first incarnation of the Dicks, which produced dizzying mayhem like *Kill from the Heart*, were authentic and bombastic while American pop music became more milquetoast in the early 1980s, awash in the soft rock of Eddie Rabbitt, Barbra Streisand, Barry Manilow, and Dan Fogelberg. And his San Francisco reinvention of the band was even more musically limber and honed.

In the late 1970s and early 1980s, punk sometimes became restless and defiant in a redneck-gone-hardcore way, especially in places like Texas, where the Dicks were the antithesis of "normal" yet were also uniquely Southern as well. Their raw, defiant, even vicious lyrics were a sore on the lip of American culture as they exposed the taboo underground—glory holes, shit fetishes, porn shops, and sucking little boys' feet. But they were also powerfully countercultural: Floyd wore Mao buttons, repurposed communist symbols in band designs, and lyrically attacked Nazis, the Ku Klux Klan, and police violence in the heart of the often-brutal South, where cowboys, sneering racists, and frat boys ruled the night. Their music—ratty, truculent, noisy, catchy, filled with bluesy howls and queer energy—proved to be magnetic, attracting the attention of Black Flag and the Dead Kennedys.

Floyd, whose voice was described by *Trouser Press* writer Ira Robbins as a "mongrel Texas blues howl," epitomized the links between the outsider ethos of the Beat Generation (both their queerness and spirituality), hippie disdain

Gary Floyd, Houston, TX, 2015, by David A. Ensminger.

for "normals," and the vexing and volatile punk era. Their raucous, bastardized version of "Purple Haze" by Jimi Hendrix, and their messy, dirty, barbed, hard-funk "Dicks Can't Swim," seal the deal. This was not a boilerplate "year zero" punk band: it was a band with a foot in the past. Even "Rich Daddy" might be imagined as a volatile, careening blues song with more in common with Howlin' Wolf than the Clash.

Also, if one band other than MDC defined the political turmoil of the 1980s, it was the Dicks, one of the anchors of the Rock Against Reagan tour, featuring acts like Dead Kennedys, MDC, and Crucifucks, which was organized by the Yippies to agitate against the conservative administration's policies and general feeling of repression. Plus, Floyd was one of the very few openly gay punk rockers in a scene saturated with righteous politics.

In a manner not that far removed from his very earthy and honest bellowing in the Dicks, he led Sister Double Happiness in the late 1980s/early 1990s, whose soulful and swaying rock 'n' roll helped continue a roots-punk movement propelled by the Gun Club, X, Divine Horsemen, and others. By the mid-1990s, his Gary Floyd Band buried deep in East Texas saggy porch howling blues, while Black Kali Ma soon followed up by unleashing a sense of Shiva as a devouring rock 'n' roll entity. Lately, Floyd has effortlessly evoked wisdom, transcendence, and transience in Buddha Brothers.

In turbulent times, when President Trump was openly sexist, gay culture has begun to blur into a gradient of "queer," and police violence is omnipresent, Gary Floyd reminds us how the punk explosion cohered a sense of freedom that is still being sought. He became a folk hero of the Left, and those who are spiritually mindful as well, but it stems from a sometimes personally painful history.

"Being Fat, stutterer is always fun . . . many days I went home crying. I hated school. Always I hated it. Never did I look forward to a day in school. I would beg my sympathetic Mother to let my stay home," Floyd revealed in an excerpt from his ongoing, to-be-published memoir sampled in my book *Austin Punk Invasion*. "I'd promise to clean the house and do anything to keep from going. I hated it. I was a terrible student. I needed to be in special ed, I'm sure. I couldn't 'get it.' The school was small town and no time to fuck around with a fat boy who was much more of a sissy than he ever knew. The coaches hated me, and I hated them. Because I was big, they thought I'd make a football player. Oh boy, was that wrong. No way. Never. They made me do the P.E. thing until I somehow got a note from a doctor saying I couldn't take it, breathing or something . . . I am not so sure that is really the case, but I was so happy to not be part of all that."

Luckily, music became a way to nurture his identity and ease the trials and tribulations.

"I moved from a very small town in Arkansas called Gurdon, and when we moved to Palestine, which was about 15,000 people, we thought it was big city. Music, very early on, played a big part in my life, and I always wanted to be in bands. I always loved the Beatles and Rolling Stones, early bands like that. The people in those bands, and movies too, played a big part in my thinking. The war in Vietnam was going on, so most of the music I liked was more in the anti-war protest vein, which shaped a lot of my alternative way of thinking. I was not much into the small-town Texas scene, and I felt alienated, but, I mean, every young person feels that to some extent."

That outsider quality, of being out of step with the community and the powers that be, could be tempered by feeling part of the larger rock 'n' roll zeitgeist, as Floyd intimately understood.

"At the same time that it was making me feel sort of out-of-whack to what was going on there, it also gave me more of a feeling of solidarity with what was going on outside of the small town. So, I never got that depressed because I knew that something better was waiting. Also, I had some friends there, and I got along with my family fairly well. I also stuttered a little bit. Then there was the gay thing. I always knew I was gay, but I wasn't always talking about it because I didn't want to find my testicles hung up on a wall someplace. They didn't like that bullshit at all, but I was able to move away to dear ol'

Gary Floyd, Houston, TX, 2015, by David A. Ensminger.

Houston, and I always felt music was my friend. If I felt sad or alienated or lonely or happy or whatever, I was always able to find music that would match the emotion. And it's still that way many, many years later."

Gary's musical wellspring had other roots too, beyond the LPs defining the counterculture's ideas and lifestyle. Unlike Randy "Biscuit" Turner of Big Boys, whose soul-punk wailing occurred alongside Floyd's own fiery yowls later at Austin gigs, the musical journey did not begin at church.

"I was in the Baptist church, but the white Baptist church that I went to didn't have singing that I wanted to take a part in. Any kind of emotion would quickly be squashed, like 'You can't sing like that!' But I didn't want to go there anyway. And then I joined the Catholic church, and they certainly weren't doing any singing either. I did like some of the chanting, though, but there wasn't enough of it. I found music more of an emotional outlet in pop culture rather than church music. Now, I've heard some wonderful church music, and I still like going, but I am more of a Buddhist type, so I do some chanting here and there."

But like so many people growing up in Texas, Black music and country music were common and frequently heard, as if ingrained in daily life.

"In Arkansas, my mother ran and managed a 'Daisy' Queen. All the teenagers would hang out there, and I would hear the music. My mother was a big fan of the blues, so very early on I was listening to blues music. We didn't really sing together, but we would listen to music together. She was a really big fan of the blues era of Ike and Tina Turner, and so was I, so we'd listen to that a lot back when Tina was bluesy. If you see the old films of her and the Ikettes dancing, they are pushing the boundaries. But my mom liked all the blues, like Lightnin' Hopkins and John Lee Hooker. They were sort of in-your-face punk rock. I think of that term as meaning very honest. And it starts with the production: these are people sitting down around a microphone. They weren't doing separate tracks. They were all playing together, so there's something very honest about that, and it offers a lot of feeling, and it was a big influence on me. As music started progressing, there were people like Canned Heat doing the blues. They did an album with John Lee Hooker, which opened a lot of people up to what John Lee Hooker was doing. I love Johnny Winter. That led me into a lot of the blues stuff."

Not to be discounted, white roots music filled his childhood as well, even if, at the time, it went against the grain of Floyd's tastes: "On Saturday evenings, there would be this long horror story for me of different country people like Porter Wagoner, Buck Owens, and others. So, it was something I was listening, also the Grand Ole Opry and Panther Hall, which had Willie Nelson. It was my young hippie days, and I hated it. But you know what, it was there, and I was listening to it."

Floyd was also living through the slow-to-die chapters of the Jim Crow–suffused South, with its ugly reminders, big and small, of white supremacy.

"My best friend at school at the time was this guy named Anthony. He was an African American guy, and he lived outside of Palestine in a small town called Tucker, Texas. It was mostly Black folks that lived there. I would go and spend the weekends at Anthony's house. He had a tiny little room that was completely filled with drums. And he was a really great drummer. This is like 1972, which to me, seems like a long time ago. It was a big deal for me, as a white guy, and for Anthony, as a Black guy, to hang out at school, and often we'd laugh about it. At school assemblies, people who were white and Black would sit in different sections of seats, but Anthony and I would sit next to each other. And one time the principal called us in afterwards and made a big deal out of it and told us . . . 'It's okay,' but we should think about that. So, I said, 'Fuck you.' It was a big scene, and my mother had to come up to school. Those are the kinds of things I mean when I say life felt a bit alienating."

But such moments helped sharpen his resolve and deepened his distrust and dislike of things immoral and racist, unfair and bigoted, treacherous and lethal.

"It started me putting thoughts down on paper to play music. Anthony and I had a band, and we played at school, and there was always a bit of controversy. We had a song called 'Why Vietnam?' So, we had to give a list of songs prior to playing, on Western Day, of all days. I wore a tie-dye shirt. We had to write the names of the songs down, and the principal said, 'You can't play this.' And we just said, 'Okay,' but of course, we did. Those kinds of things make you stronger. They may be little things, but they make you stronger. For me, it always goes back to music and painting. They are outlets and ways I can feel free to express myself."

The time was ripe, the war was in its last throes, and the sexual revolution was further expanded and redefined by queer communities as others chose the paths of marijuana legalization efforts and drug culture in general.

"At the time, people were getting drafted into the army. And there was a war going on, so it wasn't a pleasant thing. You would get a letter stating you have to report to a certain address, and you're going to be going to the army for two years. So, I got drafted, and started educating myself, mostly influenced by what was going on in music, since I didn't agree with the Vietnam War. I thought that it was a continuation of a policy that was anything but good, and our country was suffering. I decided when I registered for the army, which was a legal thing you had to do, I would sign up as a C.O. [conscientious objector]. That means for reasons of conscience that I would not participate in that war. And so, I did get drafted, they accepted me as a C.O., so I did an alternative service instead.

"They decided that it would be in Houston at a hospital called Jefferson Davis Hospital, which right off the bat is like, 'Are you kidding me with that name?' So, I was a janitor for about a year and a half. I was not at all connected to the service, except that if I didn't do my job, they would put me in jail, so I got my mop and broom. I moved there to the city, and this was an era when people were experimenting with drugs. There was a lot of psychedelics, and I was meeting a lot of young people. The whole Montrose area was very gay friendly. I didn't 'come out' for like, a year or so, because I was still living with friends of mine that I had gone down to school with, but they ended up moving away, and I knocked down the closet door and dared anyone to mess with me because I had spent eighteen years hiding something that I never felt ashamed of."

It was a decisive time that also exposed Gary to his parents' generosity of spirit, which many in Texas did not share. "I pretty much told people that needed to know. My parents were very supportive. They were Arkansas and

The Dicks and Rank and File, Studio 29, Austin, TX, early 1980s.

THE DICKS   JERRY'S KIDS

$3
9:30 PM
FRIDAY
NOVEMBER
20
STUDIO 29
(Ex- Rome Inn)

**Benefit for the
University Employees Union**

Texas people. My father could be probably more considered like a redneck. But he always supported my decisions, like when I was hanging around with my friend Anthony. An old man that lived next door to our house came over after Anthony had visited there once, and he said to my dad, 'Sam, I saw a Black guy over here. Is everything all right?' He was like, 'Yeah, it's my son's friend.' And he went, 'Oh.' But my dad stood firm and said, 'You have a problem?' And I don't recall what he said, but my dad defended Anthony. He showed another side of himself, so when the gay thing came up, he was supportive. We didn't have a chance to really talk about it because he passed away, and I was developing my thoughts and getting my shit together. But there's nothing worse than not having the support of your family when you are coming out. It doesn't matter if you are baling hay or singing at a night club. If you lose the support of the loved ones around you, it makes it really hard, and I've known a lot of people who have not had that. It's a learning process for the parents that makes it really hard on a young person coming out, whether you are in California or wherever the hell you are."

Punk rock, in essence, would later become his rock 'n' roll family and a launching pad for his untamed energies.

"When I got to Austin, I had been trying to start a blues band, but then I heard bands like Iggy Pop and the Stooges. And then there were other bands like the MC5. They were very wild, raw, and in your face, like something scratching at you. The discomfort was just enough to make you want more. Then there were the punk rock bands in England and, of course, the Ramones, and I was all ready for it. I had actually known Randy 'Biscuit' Turner before the Big Boys, and it was all around the club Raul's. I would see the bands play, and I was like, 'I can get up there and do that.' Before I even started, I would make posters because that was a very big deal. The bands who were playing would make posters and put them up around. Biscuit made some of the most filthy ones. I didn't really have a band yet, but I decided that I would make the posters for a band anyway and make up club names. I put them up all over town. People would come up to me and lie and say, 'I think I saw you, you were great,' and I would think, 'No, you didn't,' but I wouldn't say that. I would just say, 'Ah, thanks.'

"Randy 'Biscuit' Turner of the Big Boys and I would try to outdo each other, and that certainly gave the people their money's worth. Biscuit was more creative than me. He would spend hours, or days, literally, putting a whacky, carefully arranged outfit together. Me? I would throw on some torn-up dress, some nasty panties, a wig, and I was ready. But it worked, in a demented way, like an old John Waters film, live and loud. Biscuit and I loved each other. We

The Dicks reunion gig, Austin, TX, 2016, by David A. Ensminger.

both remembered the boring pre-punk time, before we had our own bands and were taking full advantage of the edgy new era. We remembered the perfectly faded denim and tousled long horse-haired boys and masturbating guitar solos. The bit of creative competition between he and I was always a fun thing, never catty, scowling, or done to be prickly and mean. Our friendship was deep. Like survivors. Being lead singers, who just happened to be gay, in popular punk bands and big showoffs too kept us close-knit."

But while Biscuit's music had an undertow of high-energy soul, hip-swiveling au go go, mutant pop, and short, sharp but still elastic funk, Floyd's had a directness and earthiness, fervent grit, like a howling preacher man unleashing a verbal howitzer, and ribald rancor too. It hit home with a newfound queer bluntness and a spirit that stretched back to scratchy 78s at the same time.

"I think punk rock is music and people got into doing it in England, Belgium, and they did it in America, so it's an international expression of music. It happens to be a common thing among some people. I always liked the blues. It's always been one of my favorite kinds of music. With the Gary Floyd Band, I actually did hard blues albums, and with the early Dicks my voice just seemed to project that, especially on songs like 'Shit on Me' and 'Shithole,' which had a little bit of a bluesy feel. When people expressed that (my bluesy quality) after the fact, I was shocked."

Gary Floyd: Heart and Mind with the Power of a Freight Train

CELEBRATING

LEFT OF THE DIAL PARTY

FEATURING

MEET GARY GREET FLOYD

Cactus Records

FREE — 5:30 PM Fri.

July 18th

All Ages

Sister Double Happiness, publicity photograph, by Delinda Vivero, SST Records.

Previous page: Gary Floyd at Cactus Music, Houston, TX, 2015, by David A. Ensminger.

Even when the Dicks were playing, people would be yelling, 'Faster, play faster.' You know what? 'Fuck you, fuck you.' To express myself through music is the most important thing to me, whether or not it lives up to some person's ideology of what I should be doing. Some songs off *These People* are rock 'n' roll songs. If I wanted to be restricted, I'd work in a gas station, or a factory. With music, if I feel restricted, then I feel like I'm not doing music, I'm doing somebody else's thought of what I should be doing, which I can't do."

In the end, Floyd is a man charged with his own sense of difference and destiny, one that veers from any path that doesn't gel with his own brand of hard-fought spirit and self-made style, all in the name of reaching unmarred authenticity, something he heard in music from the sloganizing anti-war movement to dirt-road country blues.

"I'm a musician who's made punk rock music that I think is really good, but I've also made blues and folk music. It's like when gay journalists ask, 'Are you a gay musician, or a musician who's gay?' It's like, you know, I'm a musician who's gay. And I really believe that, and they get all uptight about it. But you

Gary Floyd, photo booth, provided by Gary Floyd.

always have a few rebels, a few rock 'n' roll queers. The smartest people in rock 'n' roll are queer. I always remember that."

"From the Dicks to Sister Double Happiness, Gary Floyd Band and the Buddha Brothers, I was always happy with the music I was doing at the time, and happy that music was the biggest part of my capability to express myself. Sometimes it's 'Rich Daddy,' and other times it's a country sad song. It's all real. So, honesty is my feeling about what I've done."

5

DAVE DICTOR
My Story Is a Little Weird

MDC's blitzkrieg blend of rage and lightheartedness helps bridge the world of late punk and early hardcore to the current cultural climate and the newest crop of modern punk bands. Meanwhile, their career continues, like a stone that gathers no moss.

Ever since discovering punk's anger mismanagement, irreverent style, sexual mix-ups, and fiery political intrigues in Austin during the waning years of President Carter, Dave Dictor has become a totem of the movement by figuratively and physically trying to battle right-wing ideology—animal torture and cruelty, homophobia and sexist systems, violence against indigenous communities and marijuana criminalization, and much more. Dictor's occasional cross-dressing and showbiz goofiness, like donning Elvis attire during an entire tour, have been part of a nuanced jigsaw puzzle of his identity. And his wide-ranging lyrics, bitten by humor and fueled by passion, have mesmerized legions across the globe. In the meantime, the band's music—a motley hybrid of pure hardcore wrestling with bits of metal, country roots, classic rock, rap, and now even opera, have remained vitalized by a changing lineup.

"Chicken Squawk," a kind of rompin' barnyard hee-haw hardcore that advocates for vegetarianism, remains a crowd fave; "Acid Reindeer" is a soft acoustic serenade that addresses the hole in the ozone layer and Chernobyl; "Guns for Nicaragua" sounds like an endless rap remix illustrating the banality and errors of Ronald Reagan; and their covers aptly illustrate Dictor's affection for A.M. radio rock—"Love Potion No. 9" and "Tofutti!" ("Tutti Frutti"), among them. MDC were never business as usual.

Moreover, the band tours incessantly when a pandemic isn't grounding them, and Dave Dictor photographs the sights and people while creating an

Dave Dictor, MDC, Vinal Edge Records, Houston, TX, 2017, by David A. Ensminger.

ongoing online diary that sheds light on his keen interests, from elephants and architecture to food and customs. He has become a punk ambassador of the permanent party of dissension . . . like a seasoned, open-minded leader of the underground network where animal liberators and Antifa agitators convene. But he is also a spiritual entity, seeking to find solutions in kindness, not just in polemics.

"I landed in Austin, Texas, in 1976, and I almost immediately got a job at Domino's Pizza, one of the first Domino's. I knew Willie Nelson lived there, and I was hoping to find some of the country artists like that. I was aware of the New York Dolls, though I was not that aware of the Sex Pistols, well at least not until they actually came through Texas. I was doing this kind of hybrid country and wrote this song called "Ain't It Funny." Eventually, I wrote "I Hate Work" while on the job. I was really frustrated due to the low pay and delivering to the richer college kids and them not giving me any tips. All my songs seem to have a bit of social consciousness to them. It was not, then, an out-and-out political consciousness, except maybe a little compared to regular Nashville country-type writers."

But in his own way, Dictor was exploring the roots of both his music and rebellion, simultaneously.

"Being a child of the 1960s, the Democratic Convention in Chicago, and the end of the Vietnam War, I got educated very young about political matters, like thirteen, fourteen, fifteen years old. I went to Catholic school. I believed in Santa Claus until I was in the sixth grade. I met Jewish kids at the first public school I went to. They were like, 'Dave, we like you a lot, but there is no Santa Claus.' I remember that to this minute. I was like, 'Are you sure? Are you positive?' I was always hip to music, though. I always loved music. The Beatles were around my whole childhood, but then something happened between 1966–68, like Otis Redding, a lot of cool things in music. There were the Temptations, the Supremes, then the Jacksons, Yardbirds, the Byrds, Dave Clark Five, and it just kept going. Freddie and the Dreamers. And then I started getting into the Grateful Dead, Cream, etc. I was a young teen by then."

"I grew up with Bob Dylan's "Blowing in the Wind," Arlo Guthrie's "Alice's Restaurant," and I was a protester. I walked around my high school in 1971 with a marijuana legalization petition, and my principal called me down and said, 'Dave, how can you do this?' I just said, 'It's a free country, right? This is my political right.' I was fifteen years old at the time trying to explain why marijuana should be legalized. I had the political edge going on. I was just a kid, though. I didn't take it too seriously. I didn't think I was the next Bob Dylan or anything like that. I was trying to fit in somewhere. I wrote this song called "Ain't It Funny," which ended up being on the *Metal Devil Cokes* album years later. It just rolled out of head.

During this youthful period, he also penned one of MDC's most requested and non-traditional punk songs—a hillbilly hardcore opus to a vegetarian point of view, yet the whole thing began due to the casual but insistent request of his hardworking mother.

"Chicken Squawk" actually came about when I was thirteen–fourteen years old. I came home and told my mom, 'I think I want to become a vegetarian;

would you help me? I am not sure what I do besides eat French fries and grilled cheese sandwiches.' My mom was like, 'Oh, you are going to get weak. You need to eat your meat and eggs.' I was like, 'Mom, I want to do it. I think I have eaten enough meat. Help me at least a couple days a week.' She started baking eggplant with me—in fact, she actually started doing it vegan style. And she started making lentils and rice. She said, 'If you are going to do this, you need to do it right.' She kicked me off. She started to make my eggplant special on Thanksgiving. After a couple of them, when I endured the people saying, 'Oh, there's more meat for us now,' all of a sudden everyone wanted the eggplant. And it was a bigger hit than the turkey at the family Thanksgiving.

"My mom said, 'You write me a song about what you are talking about here, being a vegetarian, and I will buy you a guitar.' I wrote her the song with the lines: 'Bugs Bunny is a friend of mine!' My mom said, 'I owe you a guitar.' She took me out to a store for my first real Epiphone acoustic guitar. They did not have tuners back then, all they had was tuning forks. Lucky, my friend had a good ear, and he started playing guitar at the same time, and that's how it started. We were playing Bob Dylan, we were playing Grateful Dead songs, just eclectic songs in that hippie rock 'n' roll culture. Then I started slowing down and started eating meat again, but since the time I was seventeen I have stayed vegetarian."

"I was inspired by my mom, and she was wonderful woman, a reporter for the *Daily News*. She'd tell me about how she interviewed Louis Armstrong. She could be pretty straight, but she had this thing where she could be pretty cool, like taking me to see Arlo Guthrie's *Alice's Restaurant* in real time in seventh or ninth grade. She took me to see *Easy Rider* too. She probably didn't quite realize what she was doing! It wasn't that she regretted that I became a punk rocker, but for the longest time, I would be like twenty-five, and she would say, 'Are you going to be a punk rocker forever, really?' I would say to her, 'Gimme a few more years.' Every five years, she would say, 'Those few years are over,' and I would respond, 'A few more years.'"

This period became quite formative and foreshadowed his restless sense of spirit, both in terms of being on a personal journey and as part of the cultural zeitgeist.

"Kent State happened in 1970, Democratic Convention in 1968, and the whole Richard Nixon period unfolded. If you lived through it, it was a daily event of watching the news as they finally got him to resign in 1974. Gerald Ford took over, then Jimmy Carter won in 1976. I was a few years out of high school, and I went down to Austin. I just started bopping around with my

MDC and the Dicks, Barrington Hall, Berkeley, CA, early 1980s.

acoustic guitar meeting people. I went to this Chicano bar, Raul's, where they had open mic night. I was too scared to go on inside and sign up and play, but I played acoustic on the street with people that were ready to go on and do their thing. I showed 'I Hate Work' to some of the punks hanging out front. This one guy Johnny loved it. He did this version of 'Wild Thing.' So, he said, 'When are you going to get a band?' Or, 'What's the name of your band?' And I was like, 'Um, let me work on that.'"

Like many punks, Dictor longed to be part of the revolt, but he needed to find the right crowd.

"At the same time, I met Frank [Franco] Mares, Ron Posner, and we kind of hooked up with this band called the Rejects. They were friends with Bryan from the Delinquents. And he is still around. It was a fun time. We went to a few parties and played. At that time, I got introduced to the Ramones and saw them. They played a couple times in the 1970s at Armadillo World Headquarters. I saw Patti Smith, the Runaways, and Blondie. I kind of got my punk education. Then I eventually bumped into Gary Floyd. He was one of the most unique people you would ever meet. He was going out to San Francisco, and I was like, 'Really?' He had this attitude of opposition to what was going on at the University of Texas with its sororities and fraternities, the notion of success, and even the hippie thing."

Dictor had a trusted sidekick: his guitar, a gift from his mother. Few people might guess that such a guitar would gestate some of the most fierce and vehement political punk of the early 1980s.

"There I was with my acoustic guitar. I started writing one song after the other. And I wrote a version of the song 'Revolution Rock,' which made it onto a compilation somewhere, and the first versions of 'Greedy and Pathetic.' And eventually 'John Wayne Was a Nazi' came out of it in 1979. That was written entirely with my acoustic guitar. I was graduating from the University of Texas, and he died. I didn't even have a graduation gown. So, we had to sign up somewhere, and they were going to mail it us. We weren't allowed to be on stage without a gown. They announced John Wayne died, and I was there with Franco. We started singing 'John Wayne Was a Nazi.' Frat boys hated it, so we knew we had a hit [laughs]. We went from playing it acoustically to finally getting in another band and called it the Stains. We bumped around for a couple months. We were the Rejects, and then we were named something else, and then I had come up with the name Solar Pigs. We changed our name every week. Eventually, we became the Stains. We played our first gig in April of 1980. A whole bunch of MDC songs I wrote acoustically. I would

MDC and Th' Inbred, The Dry House, Morgantown, WV, by Art Reco (Bobb Cotter), 1986.

AT LAST! THE ONE AND ONLY

M.D.C.

TH' INBRED

wed. sept. 24 6pm

The DRY HOUSE

play them like that and then show them to Ron, who would then bang them out hardcore style. It stopped us from playing them acoustically and being a bunch of hippies.

"The Clash came to town, I missed that. But everyone else saw it. Patti Smith was coming around. But I was still going home to New York to see David Peel, a marijuana activist and Yippie kind of guy. He was a Kinky Friedman type of thing, a space cowboy. By 1980, I was throwing rocks at the Klan and came out with the first version of 'Born to Die' with the lyrics 'No War / No KKK / No Fascist USA.' Gary Floyd from the Dicks helped politicize me very much because he was walking around with Mao Tse-Tung buttons and talking about workers' rights in a way I wasn't. I believed in what we were saying too, but he gave such a force to it all. 'These frat boys make me sick! These sorority girls make me queer!' he would say. Just incredible. I was very empowered by that."

Then, a seismic shift began to occur: "I started writing songs about 'Radioactive Chocolate,' which came out of the Harrisburg/Three Mile Island accident. I just started writing more politically bent songs. 'Born to Die' was about the Klan and how they were killing farmworker organizers in Texas. And it was being done when I had a Mohawk and purple hair. It was a fun fun fun time. We were a pain in the ass to all the people that saw us. But we really felt we were part of the culture that was moving the barometer to a funkier, funnier place. It was a wonderful time in my life. And then in 1981, Jello Biafra got a hold of the 'John Wayne . . .' single. We sent it to Micky Creep, of *Creep* magazine, who was Biafra's roommate, and Biafra, being a record collector, opened his mail, found the record, shared it with *Maximum Rocknroll*, then the editor Tim called me and said, 'You guys are great. What are you doing?' We were like, 'We are coming to you to play.' We ended playing with Dead Kennedys, Flipper, and Black Flag, a three-day tour with three gigs stretched across four weeks. We came out west, and by that time, we were punk rockers. Black Flag had driven through our town, and they hated Club Foot [large alternative music venue that often focused on new wave acts] as much as we did, and I said, 'Hey, let me put on a show for you.' So, I put on the show with the Dicks, Big Boys, Offenders, us, and Black Flag. After that, Gregg Ginn and Chuck Dukowski were very nice to us. They opened up their tour books."

But Dictor's past had not entirely eluded him either, even as he swung through the epicenter of hardcore punk's fervent underground.

"At the same time . . . I met Dave of Reagan Youth, and I sent a letter off to Ian MacKaye. I sent a letter off to Pig Champion of Poison Idea in Portland.

I started making friends with people. We did a tour and went to NYC, where we met the Rock Against Racism people, and they talked about Rock Against Reagan, and we played with Bad Brains in Central Park. We played CBGB, we played 2+2, and a club called A7, which was a club on Ave. A and 7th. The punk rock thing just took off, and everybody in my band was like, 'Put the acoustic guitar away, Dave.' You didn't want to be discovered as a hippie wanna-be, although it was pretty clear to everyone that I was—I was a vegetarian at that point, and Franco and Ron were too. Three quarters of the band were vegetarians, and we wrote the song 'Corporate Deathburger.'

"We didn't do 'Chicken Squawk' for a while. It came out as a single, the third or fourth record we put out. We didn't want to talk to punks about being vegetarian in 1979: people would look at me like I had three heads. Everyone was very nihilistic. This is pre-hardcore, pre–Ian MacKaye. This is more Dead Boys and sniffin' glue. No future, as the Sex Pistols would say. The acoustic thing was discouraged by my band, who were like, 'Be hardcore, Dave.' I went with it, and it was a winning thing. I went out to San Francisco, and they treated me well the minute I got there. We ended up moving back there about eight months later and went on tour with Bad Brains in 1982, and that lasted for three gigs. That ended with them not wanting to use the same microphone as Biscuit of Big Boys and Gary Floyd. By then, hardcore was tough guy, Lower East Side, Agnostic Front, circular pits, and slam dancing. It was not acoustic. Not, 'I got this song about stopping nuclear power.' My band encouraged me not to do it that way. I never recorded anything like that acoustically. By 1986, I did start to do things like that, and throw a song on a record here and there. Finally, I put out 'Acid Reindeer' on *Metal Devil Cokes* in 1989."

The scene was beginning to fracture—change and fall apart, be tainted and denuded. The freedom often felt during the early advent of punk, with its anything-goes anarchic kicks and sexual nomads, had begun to close down. The religiosity of bands like Bad Brains, something they adopted *after* jump-starting their career, exposed an ugly side of misogyny and homophobia that was little different from culture at large, just as the conservative politics of band singers like Dave Smalley (DYS/Dag Nasty/All/Down by Law), Lee Ving (Fear), and Leonard Philips (the Dickies), let alone guitarist Johnny Ramone (the Ramones), which have become more apparent over time, reveal much. Punk ideology has always veered widely across the political spectrum, but often popular icons were quite comfy with right-wing attitudes, belief systems, and overall values.

Dave Dictor, MDC, Vinal Edge Records, Houston, 2017, by David A. Ensminger.

"By the mid-1980s, hardcore had started falling apart. Some bands went heavy metal, some bands started doing everything. It became more common for acoustic to be associated with punk. But still, we were on the punk rock juggernaut. I might do a couple songs on a recording, but no one was dying to hear them."

That may be true for hardcore pioneers like himself, but Billy Bragg, with his electric solo style of pro-union songs and socialist banter mixed with sentimental ballads, did find such an audience, though it might have been while opening for the Smiths, not for hardcore crowds.

"I still haven't done anything acoustic properly until *Millions of Dead Cowboys*. Forty years later, and at age sixty plus, finally I am putting something out. I would tour and do 120 gigs a year. There wasn't any time. I was exhausted. I was raising a son. All these different things under the sun got in the way. I finally did it here in the middle of Covid, when I was stuck at home, so I had time to put it out. It came out in Germany. There wasn't that big of an audience for it previously."

"Maybe in the late 1990s and early 2000s there could have been, but I was a single parent from the time he was twelve until twenty-three, and there

Dave Dictor reading at Vinal Edge, Houston, 2017, by David A. Ensminger.

was only so many hours in the day. I was working as a teacher for about eight–nine years, and sure, I picked up the acoustic guitar and played on my living room couch, but I was not going to pay for an album to be put out. Now, it is much easier. Anybody with Pro Tools can put together a pretty simple album and make it sound good. Before, it was two-inch reels and ninety dollars per hour. Analog wasn't as easy. I was living very punk rock. I was teaching in New York City, making $30,000 a year, but in that city, that is enough for rent and do your laundry and eat. I put my kid through junior college, and I got him some computer certificate degrees, and I was just focused on other things."

Millions of Dead Cowboys, his pared-down acoustic album, is a way to look backward and forward at the same time, to reinvent and reinvigorate, on a subtler scale, both sonically and economically.

"I wanted people to see the roots and the variation, and to see how the songs I wrote for MDC were written that way. I added a few of my own songs that I never put on a punk album because they weren't really punk songs. Then Mike, our bassist, added a few songs, like 'Well-Traveled Man' and 'Just for a Few Days.' I believed it was a good mix—something old, something new, something borrowed, something blue.

"Mikey [Smith], my bass player, is one savant of a musical artist. He's got fast fingers, kind of the product of the Idaho high school musical department—a very public education, very straightforward, very melody/harmony type of thing. He grew up in that NOFX/Bad Religion era, when he came of age during the 1990s. We found Chris Finster, and he has that vibrato kind of guitar. We want to be in a Quentin Tarantino movie, so we put that effect onto it. We had been working on harmonies for awhile, but it was like we want to be in *Pulp Fiction, Reservoir Dogs*, a lot of those movies. We did make it very cowboyish. Since I moved to Texas in 1976, I saw Marcia Ball, I saw Dan Hicks, and all those kind of people in Austin. I've always had that western kind of thing going on. I came down to meet Willie Nelson in Austin, I lived through hardcore, and we were able to sustain it.

"There is enough regard for the old school. People seemed to want to meet us and play with us, and buy our shirts. We just kept on going down the line. We survived. We combine audiences and get some good tours and good gigs. Then, when Trump got elected, we had the whole 'No Trump, No KKK, No Fascist USA.' The political world became so evident. And we were one of the early political punk bands. Protesters around the world were using our slogans, and people wanted to check us out again. *Rolling Stone* magazine wrote an article about us, and things fell into place. We are a band that is known two inches deep around the world."

6

JEFFREY LEE PIERCE
Ghost on the Highway

"Hardcore! We don't play anything near hardcore, those kind of people won't come and see us," Jeffrey Lee Pierce, who died at age thirty-seven in 1996, insisted to *Local Anesthetic*, a Denver-based fanzine, in 1982. In the same issue, the Gun Club is pictured holding their favorite vinyl, with Pierce clutching a Charlie Parker LP in front of the Wax Trax store window. Yet, Pierce also was known to pen reviews for *Slash* in which he exalted bands like Black Flag and the Circle Jerks, featuring his roommate, singer Keith Morris, as being akin to ". . . witnessing an exorcism" (Morris 95).

According to Morris's biography, the two would burn dried-up Christmas trees lifted from the alley next to Club Lingerie, where they had graced the edges of the stage during the season, and set them aflame in the cross streets of Sunset and Wilcox deep in the night, like a blast of sizzling fire and splattered light. And the two were also mainstays in the Bud Club, which wrapped members of X, Fear, Flesh Eaters, the Red Hot Chili Peppers, and more into their woozy revelries.

Yet, Pierce's musical prowess remains mysterious and debated, poignant and sometimes pushed off the shelf of punk by musical purists. Perhaps part of the enigma is due to his own pre-punk roots as a kid from El Monte raised by a Latina mother. These years likely shaped his outsider sensibilities long before he carved music in Creeping Ritual, an early version of Gun Club, and his deep, prolonged dive into music that was not exactly expected from a kid growing up in a town "still transforming from a semi-agrarian citrus town to a concrete-washed suburb so typical of the San Gabriel Valley" (Kokinis).

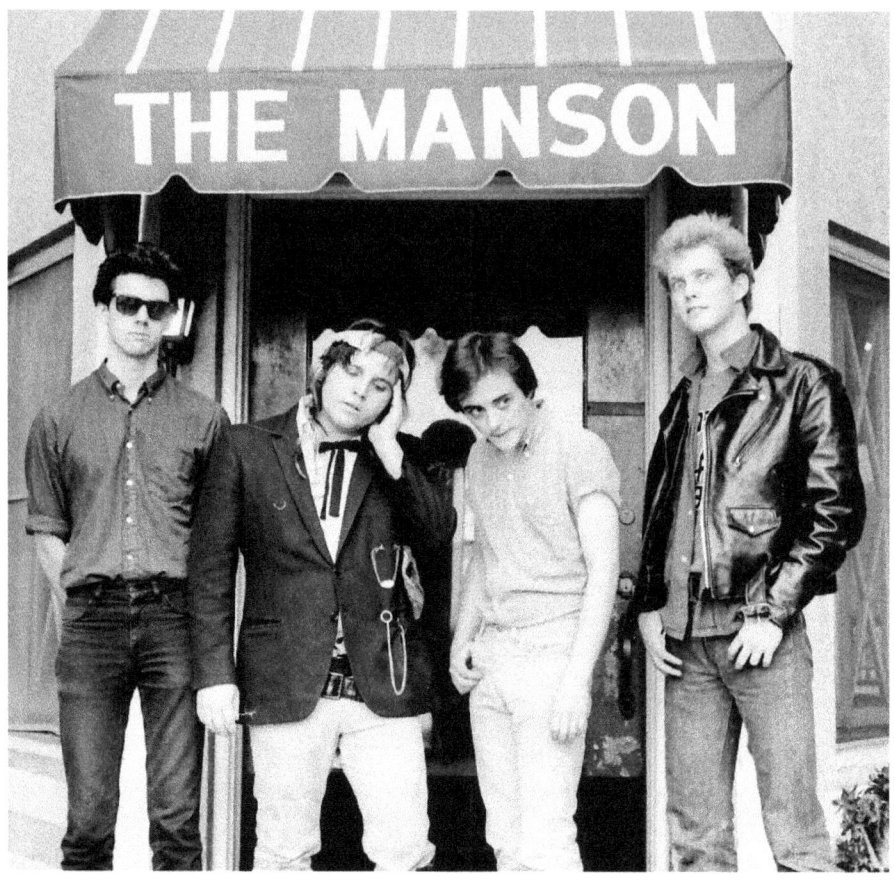

The Gun Club, by Edward Colver.

Though the roots of Gun Club seem obvious on the surface—a smattering of deep blues cross-hatched with lonesome country, western American visions, and jazz funneled through the legacy of Billie Holiday, whose "Strange Fruit" they covered, another layer seems relatively eclipsed—the Latino heritage of Pierce, and the mixed local rock 'n' roll ingredients of the California interior. According to guitarist Kid Congo Powers, this included "... oldies, R&B mixed with hard rock and psychedelic rock" ("Hollywood" 36) overheard from garages across the teenage landscape, where bands like Thee Midniters, whose wonky psych attack, cackling vocals, sweeping organ, and sizzling guitar on "Whittier Blvd" and unhinged "Jump, Jive, and Harmonize" (hard-ass psych-soul bursting with bass lines and organ rapture) enraptured relatives and kids. So did their covers like 'Land of a Thousand Dances." A live version can be heard on *In the Midnite Hours!!!* with a cascade of fan screams and handclaps.

The Latino identity marked a borderline among people, a kind of stigma. As Powers recalled his interactions with Pierce: "We bonded greatly by the 'otherness' of our ethnic background and growing up in our respective San Gabriel Valley suburbs of La Puente and El Monte. We were misfits that felt outside of our own backgrounds, but somehow drawn to it, if only by instinct, by blood—a crazy dichotomy I find many Los Angeles Chicanos feel. We didn't grow up speaking Spanish but we knew Spanish words, Mexican food, the importance of family, and customs well" ("Hollywood" 38).

The Gun Club, Hot Klub, Dallas, TX, 1982.

Pierce searched out not just different periods of music but literary pathways as well—finding modes of expression that attempt to resonate from sources that might range from Black Panthers speeches to the Book of Job in the Old Testament to hand-tilled fields in the Mississippi basin to carefully constructed verse of Modernist poets.

"Jeffrey Lee knew how to take things he loved and incorporate them directly into his work," recalls Peter Case. "He really didn't worry about having the chops. He was more of an enthusiast and conceptualist. He also had an antenna up for all things that were cool.

"I first met him at Phast Phreddie's [writer for multiple publications like *Slash* and *Rock Scene*, manager for the Zeros, and singer] in the late 1970s. Phreddie would have Drink to the Death parties, one was for Brian Jones, and one was for Charlie Parker. They were tributes to musicians, and we would just go there and drink and play all those old records. He had a small apartment,

Jeffrey Lee Pierce: Ghost on the Highway

Jeffrey Lee Pierce, The Gun Club, by Edward Colver.

and people would be packed in there. It was crazy. I went into the bedroom, and there was a guy sitting there with short hair and wearing a suit with a vest, which was weird, because that was what the Nerves would wear, and he was playing a Gibson ES-335 guitar, and just sort of sitting there playing. I went over and started talking to him, and we became friends.

"He was in a different scene at that point. He had short hair, and he seemed ill at ease. Very shy. I told him I was in the Nerves, we talked, and I think he already had a copy of the EP at that point. He was into that, we hung out, and he's the reason why Blondie ended up doing 'Hanging on the Telephone.'

"It was the summer of 1977, and we were on tour, and Blondie was on the radio, and Jack said, 'Blondie is going to record my songs.' He said that, and we were like, 'Yeah, right.' He had no contact with them: just out of the blue, he said it. Paul was trying to get a hold of them to get an opening slot on some gigs. He gave them the EP, and they told him they hated it. The manager, Peter Leeds, said, 'There are no gigs with Blondie. They are not going to play with you.' 'Did you play them the record?' Paul asked, and he goes, 'Yeah, I did. They hated it. We don't like you, so don't call here again.'

"I'm out on the West Coast a little while later, and I am in a room with Jeffrey, and I didn't even realize that he was the president of the Blondie fan club. So, he put it on a tape for Debbie and Chris to listen to on the airplane on their way to Australia and Japan. And when they got to Japan, they loved the song, and they were listening on a beatbox in the taxi cab from the airport in Tokyo, and the driver started going crazy and singing it. Like, 'I love this!' So, they thought, we have to record this because it's going to be an international hit, and it was. So, I'm not sure about that story that they hated it, because Jeffrey gave them a copy and they loved it."

Within a few years, Lee was writing tunes that caught the attention of local rockers the Last, a proto-punk band in the area.

"The first time I saw him play was in 1979," recalls Case. "I hadn't seen him in a while, and he sort seemed different. You know he had a song on The Last album, right? It was the first thing anybody recorded by Jeffrey. It's called 'Jungle Book,' a pretty cool song on a great album. The gig was at Veterans' Arena with the Mutants, the Last, Plimsouls, and more put on by a company called CD Presents. It was when we were a three-piece. Jeffrey came out when they did 'Jungle Book' and sang and played guitar. It was really cool. He still looked like he did at the party. He hadn't really gone through that transformation yet."

And the substance of his tunes was evolving, imprinted by his inner journeys, like a restless figure who seemed to seek expression beyond boilerplate punk and underground rock 'n' roll: he delved in substance more universal in scope than overheated, angsty, combat-booted teen spirit found on much material predominating in the hardcore era.

"I write a lot of despair songs," Pierce was known to declare. "They're 'Oh-God-why-have-you-forsaken-me' songs with themes about shut-off emotions and a loss of faith. That's just part of the human condition, being so jaded that the soul dies. It has nothing to do with living in Los Angeles. T.S. Eliot said the same thing . . ." (qtd. in Oliver).

Jeffrey Lee's biography is dotted with incidents that are less literary, especially at sites like the notorious Tropicana Hotel, not far from the Troubadour, with its postcard palm trees, tangled overhanging foliage, seedy allure, rusted outdoor furniture, odd-shaped pool, and televisions bedecked with coat hangers for better reception.

"The Blasters all went to this groovy, Hollywood-happening party with guys from various bands," tells Dave Alvin, "and there was these guys there named Jeffrey Lee Pierce and Phast Phreddie Patterson, who had been writing about rock 'n' roll and rhythm and blues for years. He and Jeffrey were good friends. Long story short, by the end of the night, Jeffrey Lee and Phast Phreddie are on the floor of Levi's motel room, and Jeffrey Lee broke Phast Phreddie's collar bone. He got on top of him and put his knee into his collarbone, and that was that. That's how I met him. The neat thing about the part was, we didn't know if we would fit in, because we were a bunch of guys from Downey, and we showed up and Jeffrey Lee and Phast Phreddie were sort of running the record player. Levi too. They were playing a lot of Freddie King, you know [laughs]. We felt like, okay! Turned out that the woman who had invited us, Anna, her older brother by a couple of years was a guy named Jay Statman, who as a teenager ran the Ash Grove record portion. We felt like, okay, we are back home. Then I watched Jeffrey Lee break Phreddie's collar bone."

Phast was a beloved DJ who'd spin an idiosyncratic mix incorporating Captain Beefheart and "The Loco-Motion" on any given night, and a writer and singer in the local music milieu, whose own band sometimes left writers scrambling to duct-tape together descriptions. As Shredder from *Flipside* once noted, "What do you call this brew? . . . bop, rhythm, blues, beatnik, chomp, gurgle, wack, splat." And that bone-crunching moment at his pad actually begat a friendship between Alvin and Pierce, who was eager to dig deeper into the mineshafts of music.

"Jeffrey used to come over to our place in Downey, and Jeffrey knew a lot about music, but he had this big blind spot, which was pre-war blues. Part of it was that he had a great understanding of reggae," Alvin explains. "He knew a lot about it; he could talk about reggae for hours. And Jeffrey had a great grasp on punk rock and the rock 'n' roll that was happening, whether it was in LA or New York or London or Scandinavia, wherever the hell something was going on, and he had a great grasp of pop music history. He knew rock 'n' roll history too. He came over to our house because basically he wanted to fill in the gap on pre-war blues, which we did easily. We played him Charlie Patton, we played him Tommy Johnson, we played him Skip James, and he was going, 'Oh fuck.' Because when you hear that stuff for the first time, you either dislike it or you fall in love. It's kind of like there's no middle ground. So, there were

The Gun Club, by Edward Colver.

several record parties with Jeffrey Lee, and he would bring over a cassette recorder and put it against the speaker. So, that's where he found 'Preachin' the Blues' and 'Cool Drink of Water'—from us. He had never heard it before."

"He wanted to play country blues," Case recalled. "He was learning it from Phil Alvin. He was very rudimentary at it, but he was one of those guys who picked up things quickly. Phil taught him the blues songs on 'Ramblin' Jeffrey Lee,' like the Robert Wilkins stuff. They are right out of Phil's repertoire. Phil loved Wilkins. Phil had shown him how to do 'Big Road Blues' by Tommy Johnson, so Jeffrey played these things but with a different feel. The way he played the blues at that time, it wasn't really a blues feel, it was more like a German feel. It was very different, kind of punkish and stiff. When he played solo, he would do a song like 'Alabama Blues' by Robert Wilkins, show the licks he had learned, but when he played it he would giggle. He was the only guy I knew that would do that. It was almost like he couldn't believe he was doing it. He'd play a lick and laugh a little. I used to sit around with him and play guitars, and that's what he would do."

Of course, Jeffrey was not simply somebody who home-taped, he also scoured stacks for the latest offerings of vanguard vintage tunes.

"Once he got exposed by us, he started hitting Tower Records. In those days, people like Robert Wilkins were starting to get reissued, particularly in Europe," Alvin remembers. "We had one Robert Wilkins 78, so we played him 'That's No Way to Get Along,' and again, that was mind-blowing because he thought it was a Rolling Stones song, which most people do. It was sort of like the way he taught himself about reggae, he taught himself about blues by going to record stores and buying. He would call me up and say, 'I just got this great reissue of Barbecue Bob,' and I would be like, 'Great, wow.' I never heard of Jeffrey going door to door for records. My brother and I did such things when I was like thirteen or fifteen. To me, Jeffrey might have hit thrift stores and all that sort of thing, or antique stores, but I would say a lot of his information for pre-war blues came through whatever was reissued at the time. So, he went on a crash course in pre-war blues, and it had a pretty big effect on him because it certainly lingered for most of his career. His love for that kind of music was clear. We turned him onto the book *Story of the Blues*, which came out around 1969. Our sister had graduated from high school and had gone to Europe. So, the book came out in England. On her return, she said: 'I got you this in Europe.' It was a hardbound copy of that book that she had sweetly carried around Europe for a summer. So, we turned him on to that book. Some of the facts have now been proven wrong about some of the stuff, because so much has been learned in the fifty years since the publication of the book. But it's a great book that covers just about everything you need to know."

That book became an essential toolkit.

"It's the book he pulled everything out of," Case tells. "*Story of the Blues* came with an album I had way back in my upbringing from the local public library. Jeffrey was going to London, and he gave me this book, like, 'Here. Take this. You can have it. I can't take it with me.' It was well-read. If you open it, it was filled pictures, stories, and lyrics by pre-war blues singers. Jeffrey would laugh and tell me, 'All my lyrics are out of the book. I pulled them right out of there,' and he would show me all these different places where he pulled them directly. It's funny because a little later, when I was with T. Bone Burnett, down in Texas, and I was talking to him about the book, he said Bob Dylan had a thing he called 'the book.' And for Bob Dylan, it was *Folk Songs of North America* by Alan Lomax. That's another book they had at the Hamburg Public Library that I would pour over, endlessly. In fact, on my new album, there's a song from that book that I have been playing since I was a teenager, a Lead Belly song."

Also, unlike many LA, bands that evolved, morphed, or grew into different musical genres outside the punk barrier reefs, Gun Club began as roots-punk, and its most lauded incarnation include the guitar mystery of gay youth Brian Tristan (Kid Congo Powers), mentioned previously, a fellow Mexican

The Gun Club, Starwood, Los Angeles, CA.

American from La Puente steeped in the Ramones (he was the Southern California fan club President) as well as Roxy Music and Patti Smith plus the older sounds sunk in from his older siblings' tastes, like Thee Midniters. His time spent with Jeffrey was so impressionable, even to this day, that he has released the atmospheric, jazz-shaded, hipster-shuffle "He Walks In," a tune by his new ensemble the Pink Monkey Birds that trespasses the fourteen-minute mark. It pays spiritually and musical homage to their time together as record collectors and music makers who were garage-minded and anticommercial. And the Mexican-American influence of the brown soul amalgam is not to be ignored, whether shaping the here and now or the tunes of 1980.

"We're adults now, and maybe we no longer feel like second-class citizens all the time," explained Powers to KCET interviewer and writer Melissa Hidalgo, "but the Chicano-ness does influence us. It's reflected in our love of R&B music and the blues. We all grew up with 'oldies,' music from the neighborhood and local radio. We can laugh about it now, and we can love it, too."

Like so many punks, they felt outside the mainstream loop with its consumer-minded, smoothed-out monoculture. They experienced weirdness, queerness (in the case of Powers), generative rock 'n' roll identities that led them to embrace punk's rejection of labels, as well as a basic tenacity and a hunger to leave too. Plus, they shared links to Chicano heritage, all of which blended into a sense of communitas—a not-always-obvious early mix, whether psychedelics, listening to bands like WAR, going to the Tumbleweed Theater, or not speaking Spanish at the time to later bucking the system in the punk movement (Kokinis), where their restless spirits could show variety.

"Gun Club stand out as being fully roots from the get-go," argues David O. Jones, whose father, an iconic UCLA folklorist, began driving him to shows starting with the X, Blasters, and Gears at the Santa Monica Civic in 1980. "But it's more of Jeffrey's take on blues and swampy rock than it is, say, a copy per se. He's inspired by roots, but they aren't quite his roots, and he doesn't make the mistake of trying to devote himself to remaking them. It's not quite like English blues fanatics emulating Elmore James. It's a punk ethos still in paying more homage to the form than trying to nail it down."

And certainly not every audience was left enthralled. In Houston, when the Gun Club displaced a local act for a sudden gig at the Island, crowd members threw beer cans at the band as they played, and a local fanzine writer, though enjoying the "blitzering rhythms" and "heavy, loud, thumping drum beat" overall, took the band to task: first, in the photo of Pierce featured next to the gig review, the printed rejoinder "Elvis From Hell" sweeps across the bottom left. And the review includes the acidic criticism, "As far as I am concerned, the Gun Club has too much hype and [are] worried about the right images. Saying it's swamp, voodoo music, what a crock of shit. They're from L.A. not the swamps of Louisiana!!" (X.U. 9). This was not terribly unfamiliar to punk bands; for instance, when the Sex Pistols invaded San Antonio, Johnny Rotten donned a "massively ill-fitting plaid bondage suit and a T-shirt picturing two cowboys facing each other with their huge dicks hanging out," as Sid Vicious yelped "Ya cowboy faggots"; they were met with a barrage of heckles, taunts, insults, and tossed beer cans (Young 38). In Pierce's case, he seemed to be stepping on the toes of local musical traditions rather than diving headlong into tumult.

"I do think that Jeffrey was probably trying to do something very different than the usual punk," Jones recognizes. "But he also started years after other bands, which were part of the 1977 first wave. So, his roots rebellion was probably deliberately different from the punk coming out at the time as well as early hardcore. The Blasters, of course, were always rockabilly to the core. Those were their roots, and they stuck by them. For the Gears, I think the rockabilly look was a big part of their distinctiveness, and they were coached in dressing and hairstyle by Miss Mercy of the GTO's," the all-girl group Girls Together Outrageously. "Musically, though, I think the Gears were just very influenced by early rock and roll as well as punk," whereas Pierce had his feet planted further afield.

The Gun Club, Hot Klub, Dallas, TX, by Randy "Biscuit" Turner.

To those that suggest that Pierce endlessly appropriated cultural sources for musical gain, Jimmy Alvarado has a keen counterpoint: "As for Gun Club, at least two of the members were Chicano/Latino—not to mention punk rockers, which at the time was decidedly *not* an accepted identity like it would be a decade-and-a-half later—so is it 'appropriation' when we're talking about one group of 'minority' musicians drawing influence from another group of minority musicians? Neither are part of the dominant culture. Or is it

Jeffrey Lee Pierce: Ghost on the Highway   99

a continuation of a long, very storied, complicated dialogue between two marginalized groups that has resulted in both cultures drawing influence from each other via zoot suits, 'cholo' fashion, soul, lowrider culture, and so on? Ditto for the Gears, who, to me, have always been the perfect distillation of punk and eastside 'greaser' (as in cars and DAs, not its pejorative use as a slur against Mexicanos) culture. In recent decades a variant of that Chicano distillation has found a home in the rockabilly/psychobilly scene."

In essence, Gun Club is more like an amalgam, a patched quilt, stitched from a deep emotional well, using a blend of sources culled from the contours of a man's consciousness that used history like a roadmap.

"He was very knowledgeable about the music that came out of the plantations, songs slaves sang while they worked the fields," Morris insisted. "And all those influences came together in a way that made him a unique performer" (96). And, as I would argue, they made possible songs like "Watermelon Man," not to be confused with the mid-1960s tune of the same name by Herbie Hancock. Pierce's colloquial style may seem like mimicry to some, or it may be understood, in its time, as drawing attention to the authenticity of other music and other places.

Morris is not the only person to share such accounts. Chris D. (Desjardins) of Flesh Eaters and Divine Horsemen attested to me: "Pierce could get together with Phil and Dave Alvin and really hold his own in terms of knowledge about obscure blues and country artists," he said. Desjardins joined Pierce as a staff writer at *Slash* fanzine, alongside other contemporaries like Mr. OK, Willeye, Wormy Willy Worm, and Weenieless Will. Whereas Desjardin penned reviews of Joy Division, the Standbys, the Go-Go's, George Jones, UK Subs, Bauhaus, and Holger Hiller, Pierce (writing under the nom du plume/alias Mississippi Ranking Jeffrey) dived into Big Youth, in which he describes Howlin' Wolf and Robert Johnson as "wise men," as well as Black Creole and Cajun music (under his other alias Ranking E. Lee), the New Orleans R&B of Professor Longhair, plus reggae legends Burning Spear. "He was a huge fan of that stuff," Desjardins notes, "as was Claude 'Kickboy Face' Bessy, the French ex-patriot that was the editor of *Slash*. They were two peas in a pod in terms of their love of reggae."

Pierce's earnest adoration for Black music ran deep and wide: Alvin and he shared a penchant for history, neglected genres, and artists that many punks might have shrugged off, including bygone roots tunes.

A case in point may be Alvin's album *Public Domain*. "One of the things I wanted to show," Alvin told me, "was interconnectedness; maybe that's part of the timelessness. For one, all the styles are connected, whether it's a blues song

The Gun Club, Blackies, Hollywood, CA.

or hillbilly ballad. All these songs grew up together, rubbed shoulders with each other. The other thing I wanted to show was those folksongs are archetypal, and those archetypes are still around. 'Blackjack David' may be driving a Camaro or some other muscle car, and not riding a horse [laughs]. Or 'Murder of the Lawson Family,' which is on the new record, is a very contemporary story to me.

"'Blackjack David' is a classic British folk song . . . and with a lot of them, if I were an educated man, I could make the case that they were reactions to the industrial revolution, which was a very traumatic period for working-class people. So, you have songs like 'Engine 143' about the death of the engineer. And the case could be made, if I were better at theory . . . that a lot of these songs are metaphors for people caught in the transition between the pre-industrial age and the industrial age. Right now, we're in a similar period in that people are similarly caught between the pre-technological age and the age of new technology. And in the same way that the industrial system created new classes of people, new sets of have and have-nots, technology is doing the same thing now. Any time that you have such drastic change going on, you have alienation." Pierce was similarly attracted to such themes, undercurrents, storylines, and substance.

"Jeffrey also loved punk rock," Desjardins admits. "And, of course, he was a huge Blondie fan. Most people that are fans of Jeffrey know that he was the president of Blondie's fan club, and that's how he got to know Debbie Harry and Chris Stein. He had a universal love of so many different kinds of music. He certainly had it over me, in terms of more obscure country and blues guys. I was never really exposed to his love of people like Thee Midniters or some of the doo-wop bands out of L.A. that might have posed as an influence on him. In fact, going to that era, usually when you found bands of that genre they were from the East Coast, like New York. I was personally kind of ignorant of that scene, unlike people like Jeffrey and Dave Alvin."

One of Gun Club's most enduring tunes is "Sex Beat," covered by many bands over the years, among them Two Lone Swordsmen, Nouvelle Vague, Bang! Bang!, and Alejandro Escovedo. But the song's very existence remains rather curious.

Peter Case elaborated: "At the time, everyone in LA that was in bands were having to deal with KROQ radio one way or another. Like you were going to be on KROQ, and if you weren't, you were really never going to be that popular. And if you were on it, you would immediately be rocketed to another realm of popularity. They started playing a tune like 'Are You Ready for the Sex Girls,' the worst record in the history of the world. Then Blondie had 'Sex Offender.' It was a super-buzz word to say sex.

"There were a million of those sex songs that were getting played on KROQ, so that's why I believe Jeffrey penned 'Sex Beat.' It was kind of cool, because there was this thing people called the sex beat, or fuck beat. Eddie Munoz used to say there's a Texas bluesy saying, 'the sex beat.' People had different words for it, but that's what it meant. So, 'Sex Beat' attracted a lot of attention. Jeffrey knew how to do cool things that attracted a lot of attention. Against all odds, since there was a lot of people against him. People were against him in LA. He got no respect in LA because they had watched him transform. I've been through the same thing myself after transforming from the Nerves to the Plimsouls to my solo career. When you transform, people want to put you back in the cocoon. They don't want you busting out and doing something different, like Bob Dylan going electric. People don't want you to change. Jeffrey transformed his appearance. There was a really big movie out about that time called *The Missouri Breaks*. Marlon Brando is so cool-looking in this movie. So, Jeffrey just knew how to zone onto things that are cool and put them right into his act, right into what he was doing, right into his performance. To me, that was a stroke of genius."

Yet, despite flack and criticism, Pierce cemented more friendships, often built on a mutual desire to scour history, infuse it into the present, and make music that captured the élan and substance of the tumultuous times rather than make tepid fare for radio droves.

"He was also good friends with John and Exene of X," Desjardins explained to David O. Jones in 1994, in what has become part of Jones' yet unpublished history of LA punk. "So, we were all kind of on the same wavelength. Jeffrey had an encyclopedic knowledge of obscure Country/Hillbilly stuff and blues and reggae, which you wouldn't believe. He was a real nut record collector. Just producing that Gun Club [first album], bringing that together, it was kind of a struggle trying to get that get out, having Bob [Biggs] . . . you would just really have to get in Bob's face before he'd acquiesce with Slash to get stuff out. When he realized you cared about something that much and there were other people pushing him to do it, too. It would've been nice to go in and re-record everything again, but there were already five or six things that Tito [Larriva of the Plugz] had produced with Jeffrey and The Gun Club. Sonically the situation wasn't quite as good. We ended up taking it out and remixing it with Tito and Jeffrey and I there, and it came out good.

The Gun Club, Club Lingerie, Hollywood, CA.

"I wish we had just a little more time to spend on the album," Desjardins continued, "cuz there's not a lot of bottom on the record, there's not a lot of bass. But it's still a pretty amazing record. I've had . . . more than any of my records or any other record that I was involved in—more than the Misfits record [*Walk Among Us*]—I had more people come up to me about that Gun Club *Fire of Love* record. My friend Bryan Small said that that *Fire of Love* album was the reason he moved down here from Montana to start his band, The Hangmen," who were managed by Keith Morris. "It was probably the single greatest influence on him and his songwriting. And there were so many other people I know who have come up to me—people who I have no idea who they are as well as good friends who are musicians."

And LA people sometimes shunned Jeffrey, while Europe embraced him. "Some people had a little bit of negativity," Texacala Jones reminded me, "but everybody had some sort of negativity against everybody. It's true, though, that Europe felt the Gun Club and Tex and the Horseheads were a bit more special than people in LA did because it was different for them. In LA, we were just homies. No big deal. People you saw every day. That kind of thing. Some people were disrespectful towards Jeffrey. But they were stupid. The heck with them."

It might have been due to his success with a small "s," his ongoing substance abuse, the mere fact of his mixed identity and small-town upbringing, or his deep delving into race music, but for some people, Pierce was not a hero, not an icon, not a major player . . . just a fool of sorts.

"Europe did appreciate American acts and made us feel welcome a lot, except in politics," Jones continues. "The Europeans would hate us when it came to politics. Like, they would yell at me about politics, and I didn't know what to say because I didn't know anything about politics. They would be like, you terrible, wicked, horrible Americans, blah blah blah. And I would go, "I don't even know what you are talking about. I don't believe in all that stuff. They can all go down the drain, for all I care." Then they would go, "Then you are a stupid American then." I would say, "You know, the Dutch were really successful in the slavery trade and making it possible for the new world, so when you look down your nose at me, you can thank yourself and your ancestors for slavery."

In the end, people will have mixed impressions of Pierce's contributions, but perhaps Tequila Mockingbird best summons the unfolding epoch that enveloped him: "I felt like everybody was experimenting. Jeffrey Lee Pierce was very cool to me. I never had any problems in punk rock. I find that people have quips about how horrible it was or how badly they were treated, but I think that is after 1985. I think until '85, everybody was on the same page. Since we were all experimenting with music, everything was game.

"Jeffrey told me when he was going to die. He told me when he came back from England that he was sick and he was going to die. We had been friends since New Wave Theatre, when we booked them the first time. I felt bands like the Gun Club and the Blasters were in love with the blues. They were in love with the Black artists that made the blues. It was authentic because their music was as Black as their souls. I don't believe people are what they look like on the outside, but what they look like on the inside. So, they were authentic in that way."

Perhaps, she argues, listeners should better understand the layers and complexity of the blues. "There are so many different levels to the blues. There's 'I can't find my car keys blues' and 'there's a worldwide pandemic, and I don't know if I will get out alive blues.' There's 'I ain't got no money blues' and the 'I got too much money blues.' There's the 'I don't know how I could love you so much blues,' and the "I don't love you at all blues.' I think the Blasters found their blues. Which is sort of, shall we say, 'I come from Orange County,

Target Video advertisement, from *Maximum Rocknroll*.

but I am not from Orange County in my heart blues.' X had 'I'm a poet blues . . . I am a poet and I am writing rock 'n' roll blues.' There's the 'I'm not Jim Morrison blues.' Jim Morrison had the 'I'm not Jim Morrison blues.' He was an American Indian masquerading as a white man in his body, in his skin, because in your skin you are completely different."

In the end, as she avows, "The blues is uncircumcised."

7

TEXACALA JONES
Oh Mother

> If Linda [Texacala] Jones were created by some sci-fi genetic experiment the formula would be equal parts of DNA from Janis Joplin, Marlene Dietrich, and Darby Crash.
>
> —Bruce Kalberg, *No Mag*, 1983

Just when critics imagined punk as a skinflint genre—tired, worn out, clichéd to the bone, and poor in imagination, cowpunk/roots punk erupted, creating fecund new territories. Like it or not, X mutated into the Knitters, Screamin' Sirens helped shape a new breed of irreverent alt-country, Phranc epitomized compelling lesbian folk music, the Gun Club merged Goth and twang on *Miami* and albums beyond, the Hickoids hand-mixed backyard psych rock and weird-ass redneck punk, dubbed "gonzo Jason and the Scorchers with a metal edge" (*Thrasher* 46), all while Tex and the Horseheads seemed to inhale the dust of twisted, insurgent roots rock 'n' roll, creating a sometimes peyote-like occult atmosphere that only bands like Divine Horsemen could match. In some ways, it felt like a punkified Sam Shepard play—gritty, ominous, tumbleweed strewn, and smeared with bits of voodoo.

But it all began in the foul trap of a club called the Masque—hunger games in a dark, claustrophobic basement.

"The Masque, they had cool shows, it was a great place," Texacala Jones, singer for Tex and the Horseheads and actress (*Du-beat-e-o*, *Border Radio*) recalls. "It was kinda underground. You'd go down the alley, and there were these double doors. It kind of had a little stink to it, but it sure was fun. The band that stood out that I saw a lot were the Germs, actually, the Go-Go's played down there. They were punk rock. The Plugz were down there too, and Illegal Weapon. I could go on and on, but I don't want to be a big name dropper, but a lot of bands played down there. I liked everything about the scene. I kind of don't have any favorites of anything because I just like everything at

Texacala Jones, Carousel Lounge, Austin, 2017, by David A. Ensminger.

the time I am hearing it. I've probably had a couple of favorites in my lifetime, but I am just glad to hear anything."

But perhaps little known to others, Jones's sense of roots goes beyond that realm. "I listen to jazz. And everybody says, 'Argh, I hate jazz,' you know, but I don't hate anything. But if I hear Dixieland I just get up and scratch my head and start running around like a dog chasing its tail. I don't hate it or anything, but I just get different reactions from different things."

One of her go-to artists was the leader of the love supreme, the saxophone wanderer John Coltrane. "I love Coltrane. I cannot recommend *A Love Supreme* enough! If you are having troubles way down, turn out the lights and check out Trane. He will take you away from all of it," she exclaims. "That's my recommendation. You don't have to take it. Oh yeah, fully. Trane, man. A lot of people know that words cannot describe it. There are no words for that. It is what it is."

And that sense of the soul-at-the-core, infectious spirit, and bold music likely led her to connect with Jeffrey Lee Pierce, whose affection for Black music remained undiminished. "I was standing in front of Club Lingerie. I was having a smoke. I saw this dude walking up, and he's wearing a captain's coat with shiny buttons, and his hair was glistening in the sunlight. He comes

Tex and the Horseheads, Cabaret Voltaire, Houston, TX.

up and goes, 'Hey, give me a hit off your cigarette.' And we started talking. I had just gotten off work, because I worked at that place, but we went back in and started having drinks. We got along really well, like we had always known each other. So, we started making the rounds. We had a really fun night. A couple of weeks later I saw him at a party, and we started to hook up from there because I kind of passed out at the party, and Jeffrey saved me. He was my hero. He picked me up and put me in a cab and took me back to his house where he stayed with Margie out in the Valley. I woke up and was like, 'Where in the heck am I?' But he was a really great guy . . . That's how I met him."

That sense of being simpatico with each other quickly deepened and evolved, even though Texacala was not exactly awestruck by his band. "Well, I think I had seen him a couple of times before I met him. I was going around and waiting drinks and all that kind of stuff. I saw him play at the club I worked at. I thought he was good and everything, but it didn't strike me that much because a lot of people are good, you know. I am kind of shy. I just don't go up and say, 'Hey, I think you are good, can we go have a beer?' It ain't like that. It was like circumstances that brought us together. I think we were both sort of shy folks. We didn't threaten each other.

SATURDAY JUNE 30
9 p.m.
TEX AND THE HORSEHEADS
+ KICKOIDS and DAVY JONES + IDEAS
at TACOLAND
103 W. GRAYSON
223-8406

"We would be hanging out and listening to stuff that nobody listens to, like weird obscure R&B, and we started jamming. He was like, 'Hey, I think you should play in the Gun Club.' One of the guys had left to play with the Cramps, so Jeffrey showed me Kid Congo's slide parts, and I practiced them. I did my first show with the Gun Club, and Jeffrey turned my amp way up, but I just sucked, man. I was so friggin' mad [laughs]. The band was like, 'Jeffrey Lee, it is either her or us!'"

But sometimes a door shuts and another opens, perhaps offering more gratifying experiences to unfold. Tex continues: "He had to let me go, but he said, 'we got to do a band together,' so he said, 'Let me hear you sing.' Then when he heard me sing, he said, 'Oh, my god. This is great! You are so fucking weird!' I tried out for other bands, but nobody would let me sing because they thought my voice was, well, kind of bad, but he liked it and said, 'I can work with this shit.' So, we set up a song list. He had a bunch of 45s, and we started listening to them. Like I said, they were pretty obscure. So, we started picking out songs, and we made a little set, with 'Ain't That Peculiar (Marvin Gaye) and 'I Got Love If You Want It' (Slim Harpo), which was my first recording. We recorded it, and it was featured as a flexi for *Take It!* magazine from Boston. Chris D. [of the Flesh Eaters] hooked us up with that, so it was the Flesh Eaters, Tex and the Horseheads, which was Jeffrey and me, and Meat Puppets. It was a lovely recording. I was looking for it for a long time after losing it on my travels, and it was really expensive when I got another copy."

In a roundabout way, being with Jeffrey was like re-experiencing a portion of her youth: "Well, I used to sing along to the radio, records, or somewhere—I would sing along to everything. But in Tex and the Horseheads, Jeffrey Lee and me, that's all we did was cover songs. We did 'It's-A-Happening' by the Magic Mushrooms, but we changed it all up to fit our circumstances. And we had 'Big Boss Man,' and that was like a medium-tempo rhythm and blues song by Jimmy Reed, but we slowed it way down. We pissed people off because it was so slow. It would give you a migraine. But we liked it, and that's what mattered, though I got hit on the head by an empty bottle a few times. Actually, I got hit in the head by an empty Budweiser box, and it actually drew blood. It was on the East Coast somewhere. This kid hit me with box, and I started bleeding, so I beat him up, and his girlfriend said she was going to beat me up, so I said meet me at the next day at the bar, we had a few days off. I went to the bar so she could beat me up, and instead we became really good friends and she bought me a bunch of beers [laughs]."

Tex and the Horseheads, Tacoland, San Antonio, TX.

Texacala Jones, Fitzgeralds, Houston, 2018, by David A. Ensminger.

Opportunities emerged, charting new territories for the woman whose voice defied easy descriptions but also made sense among an emergent, slippery-as-grease genre of music that her own record label described cryptically, and breathlessly, as "snaggle-toothed trashville swamp-rock blues . . ." led by Jones's "hound in hell vocals" and "non-stop orgiastic wail" on the compilation album *The Enigma Variations*.

"The guys from Enigma came to one of our shows and said, 'Hey, do you want to record?' I said okay. It was Ron Gowdy and Steve Sinclair. They had this offshoot label called Bemis Brain, so they out us on Part 2 of the album with people like Screamin' Sirens. It wasn't hardcore punk. The first one had 45 Grave on it. But cowpunk is a bigger scene than you would think. It encompasses quite a bit. Tex and the Horseheads were a kind of different cowpunk, then Blood on the Saddle was another kind of cowpunk. The Hickoids, of course, are a different kind as well. There's all different kinds."

But when Jones first encountered the term, the result was . . . chaotic: "I was in New Orleans, and I had never heard the term cowpunk, so I thought

Next page: Top Jimmy and the Rhythm Pigs, The Vex, East Los Angeles, 1981.

they were calling me cow doo-doo. I got all upset about it and tore the bar up, got into trouble for it, and had to run away from the police. It was really horrible, and then I found out what it really means, but it was too late to apologize, though. We were all friends, though."

Despite such moments, especially on the tense and confusing road, when feelings get bruised easily, the overall sense of community felt at home in LA seemed to resonate with tight-knit camaraderie. "We all knew each other. There was Top Jimmy and the Rhythm Pigs, and the Blasters, and Black Flag. Everybody hung out, though. We were all buds. We'd all go see each other's gig. One night you'd go see Levi and Rockats, and the next night you could go see Black Flag. We had a wide palette of tastes. It's a little tough at times, though. Sometimes dudes feel having to back a woman is insulting, like it's not a manly thing. Then you have to go out and drink a round of whiskey to prove you're manly and try and grow whiskers [laughs]. I just be myself now. If someone is upset because I don't have a weenie, then so be it."

Jones, in her own idiosyncratic way, creates a sense that sex roles have shriveled and need to be shunted aside. On "Short Train," she sings in a guttural bark, "Baby, thought you'd realize / I got a pair of rovin' eyes / I like to be free to roam / and call anywhere my home," staking a claim to a world she can call her own. In some ways, that kind of blunt insistence and unapologetic independence resembles hard-bitten Loretta Lynn. Meanwhile, the tempo is aggressive, and the music is an earthy, raw cataclysm of molten guitar and lurching drums.

"Lucky Hand," on the other hand, is a hell-billy special: desert-rock turned to honky-tonk shitkicker stomp making cacti shudder and Lone Star beer signs blink. Sure, plenty of bands had merged onto this sweltering highway— Lone Justice, Green on Red, Beat Farmers, and more—but none felt this feral, predatory, or suffused with outlaw tendencies.

At times, songs like "Oh, Mother" resemble the grain of Gun Club—veins of sadness and madness coat the narrative, as well as loss and grieving, and the music is an amalgam of mid-paced unfussy rock entwined with eerie acoustic fringes . . . something doomy and mysterious. "Lock Me Up" is a guttural rocker brimming with bastard-blues and raspy spoken-word (oddly, enough, resembling mid-1980s Hunters and Collectors) colored by gruff proclamations ("lock me up and throw away the key"), tidal waves of snaky slide guitar, and bone 'n' leather ambience. If Patti Smith had taken a side gig at a dust-moted, barely lit, rumpled and mildewed roadhouse in Louisiana, this might have been the result.

Tex and the Horseheads, Scream / Park Plaza Hotel, Los Angeles, CA, 1980s.

Tex and the Horseheads, O.N. Klub, Los Angeles, CA.

For writers like Andrea 'Enthal of *Spin*, the soundscape of Jones's "huge, booming" voice harkened back to Janis Joplin, and the lyrics festered like the "good-dreams-gone-bad" of Los Angeles, resulting in songs that were "raspy" as well as "burly, brawly," and "simple" (12). That is, Jones could take the most basic ingredients and weave something edgy and surreal, like barroom rock for another world.

But as much as Jones was an icon of music, she too was a fashionista, someone whose fashion drew almost obsessive attention.

"This couple Wanda and Philip had this store that was called Movie Set, and it was right across the street from where they lived. Oh god, they had the greatest stuff. They were from the old Hollywood scene, like Wanda used to dance naked on tables, and Philip would throw rose petals on her feet as she danced. Errol Flynn would be looking on. They had all these really cool stories. Sometimes they would let me get stuff and let me put it on credit. They would go ahead and let me take it out, but I got so many pretty things there, and I took Jeffrey there, and he loved it. He got some things from there. A lot of my friends that lived in the area would go there. It was a wonderful place. They had jewelry; they had everything. But they had the finger on the pulse of all the clothes that would come in and out of LA."

Even fashion was rooted in the past, whether celluloid history or religious fervor.

"My beautiful black wooden cross actually belonged to some sisters, some nuns. I think it was teak wood and had a shiny black enamel finish. It was really beautiful. I got that from Movie Set. My bone cross—a friend of mine from England gave it to me because she had three of them. She also made me a dress that had twigs, just like weird netty stuff over the dress, with twigs and weeds woven into to it, so when you would walk down the street you'd scratch people's legs, and they would swear at you [laughs]. I had a friend that wore those hoop dresses, and I was walking by her one time, and the hoop broke open and snapped and hit my leg. I was like, 'Your dress bit me!' It was tough back then, you had to rugged to be into fashion.

"The thing is, I was obsessed with it. I don't know what it is. I didn't compare it to anything or make any analysis of it. I just loved it. I loved shopping and buying beautiful clothes and wearing them, but of course they would get all torn up after the first wearing, so I'd have to go out and buy some more. I don't know what to compare it to. I would still do it today, but there is a pandemic going on."

Never sedentary or sedate, Jones has continued, unabated as an unclogged stream, producing EPs that remain pregnant with power and luster, like *Fair*. Injected with an epidemic of urgency, it showcases some of her most aggressive tunes in years, like the fiery title track that careens like a Feederz or early Saccharine Trust tune. It conjoins abrasive, rogue surf with early 1980's swift and tattered energy that blasts apart the monochrome "woesy me" music of "alt country." The tune is seriously miscreant, fierce, and heart-pounding. The other tunes, "Dining with the Devil" and "Cousin It's Cousin," are equally bewitching and grassroots-inclined. They emit loosely ambling shambolic front porch weirdness.

"I am horrified listening to my tunes sometimes because my voice is so weird, but I do love it because I can be horrified and love something at the same time, do you know what I mean? When I listen back to the stuff, I feel it is what it was. I am glad. I didn't want it to sound like everyone else. That would be boring. Everything else is already everything else. It's been done. To do something different is fun."

The *Lonely Mind* EP comes close to her first decade of output too, especially the title track's quivering, twitching-croak vocal gyrations and propeller-fast, insistent tempos; "Need No Ride" is an FM ballad hidden in imperfect warts and all disguise; and "Tumbleweeds Blues" is a misnomer, for it is crushing—a Ramones-tempo slice of raspy thunder that restores faith, while her newer tunes in Texacala Jones Pony Island Express harken back to the mid-1980s with their haunted refrains, strong guitar mesmerism (especially on the sculpted, hook-laden "Wavey" and hard-driving, bracing, raspy-voiced "Fridgette Bardot" and "Invisible Eye"), and uncanny, gothic honky-tonk rambling gone demonized punk.

"Well, I think people should be nice to each other and not yell at each other. That's possible. I hate when people are mean to each other. I believe in all the good stuff and all the fine wonderful thing the universe can be, and all the other stuff will go into a black hole and get reorganized and turned into something good. So, all the people with evil intentions will get sucked into the black hole and turned into new fresh spirits. That's just a theory. Everybody will end up in the black hole eventually."

Decades may fly by, the winds of time may curl back one's ears, one's hair may spot with piecemeal gray, but inventive, singular women like Jones don't grow old, quiet, and weary: they strike with newfangled determinism and backbone. It's not reinvention on her part, but a return to original fortitude and an offbeat sensorium—music that is left-field, veering, bone-chilling, deadly honest, and never boxed-in.

"I will always love music. Sometimes I can't listen to it late at night, when I try to sleep. So people try and listen to music, but if I listen to music, it makes me want to get up and dance, then I can't get any sleep."

8

CHRIS DESJARDINS
A Hard Road to Follow

When a band as enigmatic and elusive as the Flesh Eaters reemerges from the shadows and stalks America, as they did in an unexpected tour in support of their 2019 album *I Used to Be Pretty*, any music enthusiast who leans into punk should take heed.

Throughout the late 1970s and into the mid-1980s, Los Angeles became defined by a melting pot of tribes and subcultures, and the Flesh Eaters formed part of the prescient, dark, roots punk core that also gave rise to the Gun Club (whose signature tune "She's Like Heroin to Me" they cover), Tex and the Horseheads, and others. In doing so, the Flesh Eaters marked a gritty, luminous path that few can match, which at times seems reminiscent of outlaw film directors.

"Well, the difference with those movie guys is that they did conform to a lot of genre stereotypes and tropes," explains Chris D. (Desjardins), singer and mastermind of the band, "but the best directors worked around them and added their own quirks to the stuff that made it unique. I think any art form, it's that old cliché maxim, you have to know the rules before you can break them. And when you are given a set of rules or a structure, actually I think it's a good thing if you can bend the boundaries and break the mold to some extent. I actually like genre films because they have that structure, and I like to see how inventive directors get around those boundaries and those restrictions by adding their own vision because the best of those filmmakers really created some wildly original pieces of art that still work within their genre. With music, it's a little different. But yeah, the analogy is there."

I Used to Be Pretty forages through their catalog and grabs musical hostages from their lauded earlier albums and re-cuts them for a strange new

The Flesh Eaters, *A Hard Road to Follow* album advertisement, 1983.

century. But the Flesh Eaters are certainly not refrigerated relics; instead, they remain an open gate to the netherworld: roiling, menacing, and eerie.

"There are times when I really wish I had not called the band the Flesh Eaters because it gets automatically gets stuck in that, 'O God, I don't want to listen to some band called the Flesh Eaters,'" says Dejardins. "But there are a few other bands that have names like that. I originally had a few other names for the band, but I was being very much, 'everybody gets an equal say.' Some of them were pretty nondescript, but there was one that was a title of a Big Youth album that I loved as a name of a group, which was Screaming Target, but I don't know how much more acceptable that is compared to the Flesh Eaters. But the Flesh Eaters always conjures up horror movie imagery, and everybody always thinks I took it from a black-and-white, early 1960's horror/sci-fi movie that was quite gory for its day. It was like an indie movie made by Jack Curtis.

"A lot of people think I took it from that, and I am a fan of that movie, but that's not really where I got it. I was more into using the name as a descriptor of prehistoric times, you know, something primitive, not necessarily horror movie imagery. But then again, there's so much from *A Minute to Pray, A Second to Die*, and some other Flesh Eaters albums, that have had horror movie imagery. But it's not the same kind . . . I love the Cramps, but it's not the same type of tongue-in-cheek horror movie imagery that the Cramps did, and did very well. Because there are other bands which I will not name, that have used horror movie imagery, that I think are kind of . . . just lame, corny."

Desjardins has remained as unique as Nick Cave. Both are beguiling figures cut from a similar cloth—intellectual without being wooden, highly charged without being self-destructive, and just sinister enough to keep a listener's pores puckered, with a tinge of politics beneath it all.

"There's so much political, and I don't mean left or right political thinking, behind my lyrics that I don't even think about it anymore. There's a lot of sexual politics and a lot of truth telling and soul bearing that kind of doesn't worry about the consequences of speaking out, and that is because I have always felt that art needs to be honest as far as the interpreter. I always end up going back to Symbolists, nineteenth-century France, like Baudelaire, Rimbaud, and Octave Mirbeau, the author of *The Diary of a Chambermaid* and *The Torture Garden*, who were very subversive in just the way they looked at life without a set of ground rules that society had set up to try and keep the population under control. So, that is always kind of a subtext. I look at politics from the standpoint of a poet first. . . ."

Like a margin walker exuding hard-bitten attitude, Desjardins blurs boundaries, splicing together an early lust for punk life (a la groundbreaker Patti Smith and French writers) with an encyclopedic knowledge of film, music production chops from his time spent on albums by the Gun Club, Dream Syndicate, and Green on Red, as well as his own metaphoric sensibilities. And the sense of place matters much as well, the loss of which he bemoans: "But there was this seediness about Hollywood that I loved, and the kind of trashy Times Square ambience of Hollywood Boulevard in the early 1970s when I was in college. I wasn't living in Hollywood, but I would come to Hollywood all the time because there were movie theaters all the way down Hollywood Boulevard, some of them open all night, a few others that were open until three in the morning, every night of the week. There was a tremendous influx of all kinds of movies from all over the world, both highbrow and especially lowbrow sexploitation, especially Euro-trash cinema, both horror and sexploitation. And there were a ton of biker movies and all kinds of genre movies that were lurid, excessive, but tremendously entertaining to watch. And you could see so many different types of films, and I loved that part of Hollywood, and it gradually eroded."

Few people might guess the records that were filling the nights at his premises, a bewitching tangle of aural roots pulled up from years of collecting: "The Peter Green era of Fleetwood Mac. By 1978 and '79, I had heard the Sonics because this reunion era line-up of the Flesh Eaters were covering 'Cinderella'

The Flesh Eaters, *A Hard Road to Follow* album advertisement, 1983.

The Flesh Easters, by Edward Colver.

in 1981, and we didn't record it for that *A Minute to Pray, A Second to Die* album but we did it in the six or seven live shows we played in 1981, so yeah. I did have those records. So, as far as the predecessors to the punk scene on the turntable, I had a lot of . . . well, if you are talking about classic rock in terms of the Rolling Stones, I had all the Rolling Stones records up to *Goats Head Soup*, but I wasn't a very big fan of that record, so I sort stopped there. All the Velvet Underground stuff, all the Stooges records, the New York Dolls albums, all of Bowie's albums up to *Low* or *Station to Station*. I don't remember which one is the later one. They were right in a row. Those were the last two Bowie records I got, but I got everything before that by Bowie. I was a big fan of his. I was a big fan of Neil Young as well. *Everybody Knows This Is Nowhere*, I loved. There are so many other bands from the 1960s—Jefferson Airplane, especially *Crown of Creation* and *Volunteers*, I was a big fan of those.

"But I was also a big fan of a lot of soul music. I had James Brown albums, at least five or six Al Green albums, a couple of Van Peebles albums. One of my girlfriends was a big fan of Rick James [laughs]. I had the album with

'Super Freak.' I had some early rap albums from the Sugar Hill people that were quite entertaining, and I enjoyed them a lot. I really can't stand rap now, it's a rare exception when I find a rap song I like in this day and age. I had an eclectic bunch of music. That being said, writing for *Slash*, I was constantly exposed, and often got promos, of 45s of American and British bands, a lot of that wave of British punk and American punk that came out in the late 1970s that I was a big fan of. Some of them I am not as crazy about now, but some of them have kind of retained their attraction to me, but some not so much.

"The other person that easily comes to mind almost immediately is Roky Erickson. I liked the 13th Floor Elevators, and I loved the Roky that was around and making records in the late 1970s and early 1980s, the "Cold Night for Alligators" and "Two-Headed Dog" kind of stuff. He was somebody that was definitely in touch with another dimension in the best possible way—the dimension of his psyche. I am a huge fan of David Lynch, and he talks about ideas catching the bigger fish. I really relate to his ideas about how inspiration and how ideas for creating things bubble up, and you have to let them bubble up from the consciousness and subconsciousness, and if you let them come up, and you don't try and force them, you find an enormous sea of possibilities, as Patti Smith might put it. Roky was really tuned into that."

Desjardins's own writing process, and his ability to stitch together a band, seemed a bit mystifying, off-the-cuff, and unique. "John [Doe] and I became pretty good pals quickly, and Chris at that time was John's best friend," recalls Dave Alvin. "I was familiar with Chris because of his writings in *Slash* magazine, and from the 'Pony Dress' single, which I think came out on Rik L Rik's label. I'm not sure. In those days, if you were hanging out and getting drunk with John, you were also hanging out with Chris, so when Chris came up with the idea of doing an album, Chris saw something in me the way I played guitar that would be great for this new version of the Flesh Eaters. And John agreed, and the next thing I know I am at Chris's apartment off of Fairfax, the three of us are sitting there, and Chris has been driving around LA with a cassette recorder next to him in his car, and he sang all the songs for that album. He was writing them in the car. The three of us were standing there listening to his tapes with all the sort of traffic noise in the background and Chris sort of making the sounds for the different parts. Chris gave us each a tape, and John and I decided, okay, you take these four songs, and arrange them, and I will take these four-five songs, and arrange them, and then we'll take them to the band.

"Then Chris asked Bateman, and John asked DJ, because at first I think the idea was to have two drummers, and then it became, no, I will play marimbas

Flesh Eaters, Clutch Cargo's, Detroit, MI, 1980s.

instead," Alvin continues. "Then Berlin went and started playing with us, but he was playing with a variety of bands in town. Typical Berlin. I am not sure if it was a mutual revelation on the part of Chris or me, like 'Hey, you know what would be great on this? Saxophone.' One of the songs I got handed to me to arrange was 'Divine Horsemen.' I heard the Coltrane-esque little line, and I just thought, there is a Coltrane meets New Orleans/Bo Diddley thing going on in the rhythm section, then the guitars and bass, so all we have to do is rumble. But if you had that Coltrane-esque kind of wispy thing going on above it, then it might be kind of cool. The first time we rehearsed it, it was like, 'Yep, that's it.' It's weird, and it's different than anything anybody in LA or anywhere else was doing. So, we felt, 'Let's go for it.'"

Blues was always an undercurrent as well. "There is Lightnin' Hopkins and so many other blues guys that I am crazy for, like the Chicago blues, like Howlin'

Wolf and Muddy Waters," says Desjardins. "But there were a lot of country blues guys from Texas and Louisiana. I am a huge fan of Clifton Chenier, the Cajun style of rhythm and blues. It's funny, because with a lot of those blues guys, I wasn't really thinking about where they were from when I heard them. John Lee Hooker is another one. I love his stuff, especially his very late 1940s and early 1950s stuff that sounds like he's recording in an underground mausoleum or something. I love that kind of sound, that basic primitive sound—the kind that raises the hair on the back of your neck when you listen to it."

And when it comes to the notion of cowpunk or country-punk, Desjardins notes both the ludicrous notion of such a genre or category but also the hard fact that a varied milieu of sounds was emerging: "In late 1983, I had really grown tired of playing deafening music at full volume all the time, which is what the Flesh Eaters had become by then. There had been a transitional album, *Forever Came Today*, after *A Minute to Pray*, which didn't have any of the *Minute to Pray* guys on it. Steve Berlin came back to play sax on a few songs. That line-up did another album called *A Hard Road to Follow*. Even though we had a couple of Memphis soul type covers, we did an Al Green song and a Van Peebles song, we were still pretty over the top in the volume department. It was impossible to get my guitar player to turn down his volume. There was some internal strife in the band, not with me, but amongst the other three guys. I just got sick of it. I wanted to do something that was more laid back and song-based. I was listening to a lot of country.

". . . there really wasn't anybody copying other people, at least within the scene. We might have been emulating country and western music, but it was electrified to a great extent, but it was influenced by 1960s and early 1970s country, which was still within the realm of great songs still being written. I think that that had gotten completely homogenized and diminished by the whole country music machine in places like Nashville during the late 1970s, it really started to disappear. By the 1980s, there was very little that was coming out from those purveyors of so-called authentic country that was identifiable, at least by the people I knew, as country music, anymore. In that way, we were very retro, and I would not say close-minded, but real purists."

Flesh Eaters, Anti-Club,
Los Angeles, CA.

9

RANK AND FILE
The Conductor Wore Black

> Nuevo-country bands are popping up left and right in Rank and File's wake.
>
> —Michael Hall, *Trouser Press*

Just as hardcore began to drench the stateside scene, often bulldozing through the punk sense of weirdness to create boilerplate sound and fury, Rank and File, whose core makeup remained the Kinman brothers from the fiery Dils, emerged as a counterpoint. At the very height of vitriol-filled hardcore (rage as a form of epidemic), the Kinmans revoked their punk and headed south to Austin, Texas. "Later you had a bunch of people who were aping a generalized form of punk rock appealing to disgruntled suburban youth . . . a subgenre of punk called hardcore. There were no ideas in it at all. . . . In the original punk rock it was very much a cross-cultural blending and pollinating," the Kinmans explained in *Punk '77* (92). In Texas, they helmed Rank and File with punk peer Alejandro Escovedo (originally, Chip and Al formed it in New York City, but they soon decamped to Austin, where they were joined by Tony) from the Nuns. In doing so, they opted for restless, sincere, stripped-down twang that felt more like a sawdust-smattered dance floor in Lubbock than the dank graffiti dens of Los Angeles.

"My folks would listen to country music on the radio," recalls Chip, "like when we were driving in the car. And I don't remember any song, well, I vaguely remember 'Detroit City,' but the song that sticks out most in my mind is 'White Lightning.' Mostly because I thought it was funny. So, it stuck in my mind and really became part of me. And then my father, when he got back from Vietnam, he had brought back two Japanese Johnny Horton records on colored vinyl. I really thought, and I still really think, those are good records. So, that was stuff that I absorbed. I really didn't start buying records until I guess around 1971, when *Who's Next* came out. I saved my money, and I was

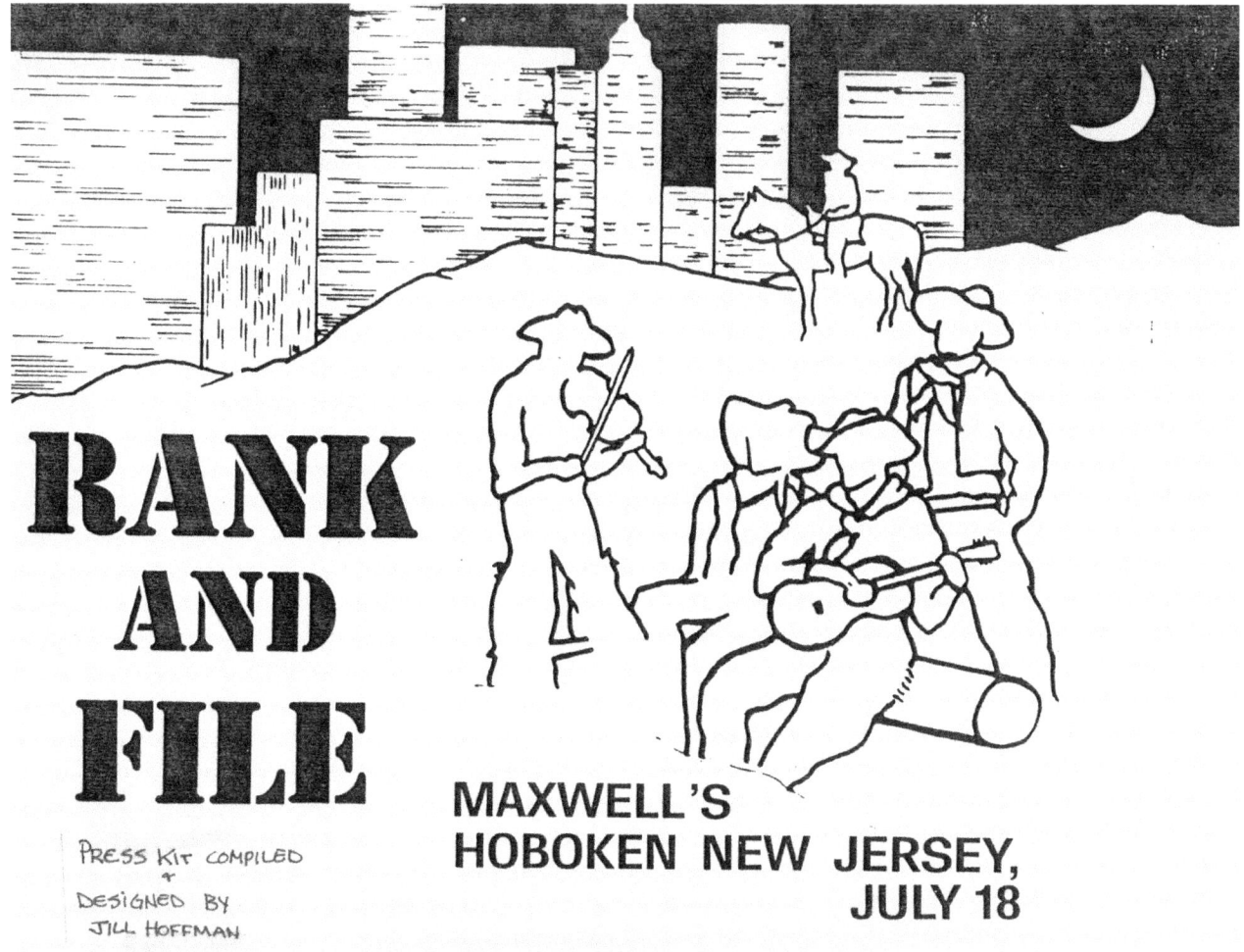

Rank and File, Maxwell's, Hoboken, NJ.

going to buy my first album. And I had a friend that had a copy of *Woodstock*, and he really liked Ten Years After's *I'm Going Home*. So, I was familiar with that and the Who because my brother Charles had *Live at Leeds*, and I thought that was a really neat record. So, I went to the store to buy a record and *A Space in Time* by Ten Years After had just come out as well as *Who's Next*, they were both brand new. I remember holding both of them in my hand and going, 'Which am I going to buy?' again and again. Luckily, I bought *Who's Next* [laughs]. I bought that, and from there on I was the world's biggest the Who fan. The only time I cut school was to buy *Quadrophenia* the day it came out. I used to walk to Leucadia from Carlsbad, which is about five to seven miles, and I used to walk to a record store there and go through their records and hope they would have copies of *The Who Sings My Generation* or *Happy Jack* or *The Who Sell Out* would show up in their record store because at that point those records were old and somewhat obscure. I did find them there, so I was stoked."

But the arc of his fascination plowed through musical fields even further back. "I love Little Richard, Jerry Lee Lewis, all that early stuff," admits Chip Kinman. "Those are great, great, great records, and I have always really loved

Rank and File "Amanda Ruth" 45 (Alejandro Escovedo on left), Slash Records, 1982.

initial explosions of music. The first reggae that came out, the first rock 'n' roll that came out. For that matter, the first romantic classical music that came out post-Beethoven. Wagner and stuff that's new, like punk rock, of course. When it's new and exciting, that's what I always go to. Country music, new and exciting, that's what I go to. Once it's been recycled a few times, sometimes by me [*laughs*], I am not as interested. The first inklings get my interest. The people who maybe knew what they were doing or didn't know what they were doing, but they created something."

Like so many roots punks, taking one step into the scratched past mattered mightily. The Dils transformed from fiery Communist punk firebrands to being an exemplum of roots-pop, especially as they forged Rank and File. Their album *Sundown* featured such hummable tunes as "Amanda Ruth," which sounds almost as barebone, melodic, and ear-friendly as any 1960's country AM radio fare. The album featured "all the tongue-in-cheek naivete and twangy guitar" but never lost their wit," *Playboy* argued, and the notions of "work and rage," perhaps traits expected from ex-punks, only existed "nominally" (30). The punk edge gave way to more subtle wordplay, perhaps echoing country greats.

"We listened to the people who invented the stuff, so we'd keep going back," Chip notes. "I'd listen to Merle Haggard, and I'd go, this is great, then

Rank and File: The Conductor Wore Black   131

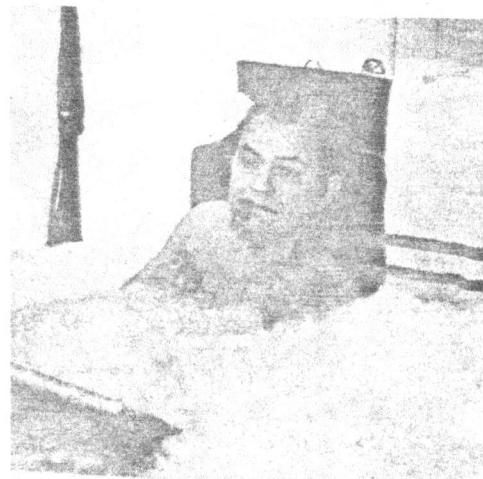

RANK N FILE at DUKE'S
THURS · JUNE 4th
w/ the RIVALS ← SR&R

someone would say, hey, Lefty Frizzell was his big influence, so I'd go back and listen to him. And I would go, ah, I can see where he got all that. And then I would find out Jimmie Rodgers was Lefty Frizzell's big influence, so I'd go listen to that and keep going back to the beginning. That's what we did. I had no interest, and I still have no interest, in hippie country. I do not care about the Eagles, the Byrds, Poco, Flying Burrito Brothers, any of that stuff. I wanted nothing to do with that. That stuff left me cold, and it still does. I like a few of the Byrds' psychedelic hits, but their country stuff I cannot handle. We were listening to Merle, Waylon, Lefty Frizzell, Willie, Cash [note: his tune "Guess Things Happen That Way" was banned by the BBC in 1958] . . . people who were bucking the system. That was appealing. Their orneriness came through in their music as well as their attitude. We heard power in the two-beat sound."

Yet, some critics could not handle Rank and File. In an expose on country punk published in 1984, writer James Marshall shrugged them off as "custom made for rock critics who also seem to like to bring their guilty white liberal petty ambitions into rock 'n' roll as a way to justify big words . . . And they can't play worth a wack either" (13). Yet, anyone that knows the Kinmans understands their disdain for pretense and people who "put on airs," profit-minded music business matters, bloated critics, and regurgitating radio hit factories. In fact, at the time Rank and File appeared, they were like a sonic island, uninformed and untouched by the contemporary country scene of Alabama, Ronnie Milsap, and the Oak Ridge Boys.

"We never listened to that stuff, and that stuff was never any influence at all. But, between old classic country and somewhat contemporary, was outlaw country. It was a newish thing, spare, not a lot of trickery in it, as a lot of the standard country did, or what was popular at the time, like *Urban Cowboy*, and that sort of thing, Of course, you listen to that stuff now, and it sounds like the Carter Family. Outlaw country really appealed to us, stuff like 'Red-Headed Stranger.' It's so spare and so great. Also, I love the story of Willie Nelson handing in that song to RCA Records, and they thought it was a demo. They were like, 'This is fine, when do we get the record?' He was like, 'This is the record.' We really found the power and the strength in that sort of early country as powerful as 'Anarchy in the U.K.' It was just different, but just as powerful.

"And when we did 'The Wreck of the Old 97,' well, that song is extremely fast," Chip recounts, "so it was a natural for punks. I'm not sure the punks knew they needed or wanted country music, but as it turned out they did. In

Rank and File, Duke's Royal Coach Inn, Austin, TX.

Tony Kinman, Rank and File, by Edward Colver.

Rank and File, we believed we were playing country music and not a variant thereof. Austin gave us a home to do that, plus we ate some really fucking good barbecue! The Dils covered Buddy Holly and Velvet Underground because those two bands were so important to us. We discovered them when we were exploring the roots of music we loved. Something we always did."

Soon, the band had toured, cut albums, and gained press attention, but other matters still nagged them. "We made three Rank and File records in big studios, all with producers, everything was fancy. We were finding what those roots were, what was something that meant something to us. Also, what was a bit part of the equation was, and still is, do I have anything to add to this? I can listen to it, but can I add anything to it? Can I add my voice to this sound, to the feeling, to the genre? If we didn't think we did . . . well, when we got into a territory where we didn't think we had anything to add, or push it forward, we were in trouble, like the third Rank and File album. There are some nice tunes on there, a few good melodies and harmonies, maybe a few clever chord changes, but that doesn't make an album. We would fail if we

Next page: The Dils, *Search and Destroy*, No. 7, 1978.

SEARCH & DESTROY

No. 7 $1

dna

devo

subway sect

roky erickson

cabaret voltaire

tried to get above our reason. It just wasn't really something we could do. But by the same token, I don't mean to use a threadbare phrase, but we didn't try to hide our talent under our bushels. It's like, okay, we can listen to the music, then ask, what can we do to take it to someplace even further, and let's do it and be proud of it. Let's go forth.

"It's funny, I was going an in-store for the John Doe book [*Under the Big Black Sun: A Personal History of L.A. Punk*], which I wrote a chapter for, and we were down in San Diego. There were all these people, and we were signing books and stuff, and we're talking to the people who were there, and someone asked, 'Hey, did you know what you were doing while you were making these records?' John Doe said, no, we didn't know, we were just writing and being in a band. My reply was yes, we knew. We knew every step of the way. For punk rock, for Rank and File, for Blackbird, for Cowboy Nation, we knew we were doing something radical, and we leaned into it. We were real conscious of what we were doing, though hopefully not overly conscious because that shows. And we were conscious of what we were trying to do; whether we succeeded or failed, time will tell."

10

PETER CASE
Beyond the Midnight Broadcast

Artful, poetic, and ever-shifting, Peter Case is a transcendent emblem of American music, a haunting spirit letting songs dwell deep. In doing so, he distills from the mind-bending acid rock of his youth, earnest and earthy folk twang, stark and lean punk, and deep bellowing blues, just to name a handful. Even within the last decade, he has cut impressive, prescient albums, like *Hwy 62* (for which I shot the back cover photograph), an album that explored Pelican Bay penitentiary, plus a highway full of lore that cut straight through small-town America, immigration, and more. African American/Jewish/Cherokee songwriter Ben Harper dubbed it "a lesson in songwriting . . . just a master class" (qtd. in Zollo). No wonder he plays on the album as well.

Case has always been poignant, relevant, and sharply attuned to the complicated world of underground music. As a late 1960s teen, he sought out bluesmen and gigged with anti-establishment schoolmates, like a scruffy hero behind buzzing chords. Case has witnessed so much, including the musical upheavals of the 1960s in his hometown of Buffalo.

"When I was around four or five, right as my sister was listening to rock 'n' roll, I just really loved it. I don't remember so well. I had a ukulele and was trying to play it, so I'd run around and bang it all the time. The Kingston Trio were happening when I was five," Case recalls. "I made my mother buy me every record. That was before the Beatles. They were fantastic. They sang about death and the sea, and did calypso songs. But the things that put me on the path I'm on now were the records of Mississippi John Hurt. In 1968, I heard his record *Today* on Vanguard."

Peter Case, Mucky Duck, Houston, TX, 2017, by David A. Ensminger.

And a trenchant sense of place has inundated Case as well: "Buffalo, where I grew up, has a big local blues thing going on, which I was part of. It was like Detroit and Chicago. A lot of people came up from Mississippi to work in the factories. There were people like Elmore Witherspoon that played blues, who would come over from his shift at the Ford plant. The Band knew all those guys in Buffalo, and that whole style of music was passed down to younger players. I came up in the scene playing piano when I was fifteen.

"Before that, when I was a kid in Hamburg, New York, I had a four-piece band, and I was super into Doug Sahm. I was thirteen or fourteen, but I knew guys like him and Bob Dylan would cut old blues songs. So, I was like, I am going to do a song by a blues singer, so I learned 'When I Was a Cowboy' by Lead Belly. Then I did a Tex-Mex version of it with a groove to 'She's About a Mover' by Sir Douglas Quintet. This is one of the ways that music comes together."

Next page: The Nerves, Denver, CO, 1977.

For people like Case, American music is a patchwork that can be woven together in endless variations by those willing to reimagine both the music and themselves. Plus, just as young bands build a repertoire and grip a vision of the future, cutting their teeth on tunes in which their chops emerge and get honed, they also build a sense of social intelligence and togetherness, a way of being.

"Nobody understood what we were doing in Hamburg back in my high school years! I recorded it on my album *The Midnight Broadcast* the exact same way we used to do it. This was how you used to be able to learn about roots music. You learned from people who knew how to play and loved it. So, I learned from guys in my town, then when I came to San Francisco, I learned from people like Michael Wilhelm that had learned from Mance Lipscomb and Walter 'Brownie' McGhee. We would go and see people like Sonny Terry and Brownie, and you would learn so much by just watching people."

In the dank and dark clubs full of shadow play, seemingly endless songs, and swirling cigarette smoke, youth like Case listened not just to chord progressions but also to the way people discussed the music on and off stage, creating lore and a sense of history. Often quite suddenly, those youth get restless. No longer content with being mere faces in the crowd, and emboldened by desire and tenacity too, they jump up and become music makers themselves.

"I left school when I was fifteen," says Case, "before it was even legal, and was hanging out with musicians in Buffalo. I'd be the youngest member of the bands; everybody in the band would be like thirty. They really didn't have songwriters there to lead the charge, but they had the most incredible piano players and guitarists. Van Morrison would come through and pick up people. It was pretty well known because at one point John Lennon was even coming over and looking at the bands because of Ronnie Hawkins, or so I heard. I had the good fortune of coming up through that scene. Back then, there was a different role for every instrument in the band. There was a rhythmic structure; it was not freeform. There was a whole way of working together that was dynamic and exciting.

"I formed Pig Nation at the age of fifteen in 1969. I was already a participant in the anti-war movement, and [we] attracted some attention for our radical anti-status quo antics. I'd left school after completing ninth grade and moved in with a bunch of like-minded young freaks."

Case's experiences speak to an essential otherness—that sense of being out of the mainstream loop, disenchanted, like an underdog or margin walker, and averse to suburban norms and a stultifying consumer way of life. "I was

Plimsouls, Culver City Veterans Auditorium, CA, 1980.

a weird kid. I wasn't necessarily working class, except that I dropped out of high school and left my parents. I was almost what you could call artist, runaway, or marginal class. My parents were middle class. My parents both worked. They were each in a union. At one point, my dad had a little ice cream stand, but that's not like working at the steel mill. Whatever it was, I didn't get along with it, so I left at the end of my fifteenth year. I like what Donovan says, 'Seven percent of people are bohemians.' They read, and they are into the Beats, poetry, blues, all that subterranean hum.

"My political attitude was formed by growing up in the years of the civil rights and anti-war movements; watching all of our greatest leaders get murdered; the lyrics of Bob Dylan, Frank Zappa, Jefferson Airplane, MC5, and Phil Ochs; the music of the Plastic Ono Band and Captain Beefheart; and the books of Allen Ginsberg, Abbie Hoffman [*Revolution for the Hell of It*, *Steal This Book*] and reading *Ramparts* magazine, a radical monthly, which at the time was available at newsstands coast to coast. I was also a big fan of deep blues and country blues musicians, which led me to conclusions at odds with the prevailing culture."

Then the road called him to the western fringe of America. Case soon immersed himself in San Francisco street life, a singular and fervent kind of subculture. "There's something about the West. San Francisco is a Wild West town, a gold rush town. When I got there in the early seventies, it still had a wide-open Western feel. There were people from all over the country there, as if somebody had tipped the country, and everything that wasn't nailed down rolled out to San Francisco. There were all kinds of people on the street playing folk, blues, and country music. The San Francisco rock movement—the 1960s one—was completely founded on folk, country, and blues music. The Grateful Dead were a jug band, the Charlatans were basically a ragtime band, and the Jefferson Airplane was founded by guys playing Reverend Gary Davis. Even Skip Spence from Moby Grape was playing country and folk music, so it was all really grounded in that. You also have to look at the Berkeley Free Speech Movement.

"By 1975, everything had changed. These were the *dark ages*. The music had disappeared. I felt stranded there musically and culturally. As we started the Nerves going, it was in a rock 'n' roll vacuum. There were no venues for people our age. One of the only places we could play was The Garden of Earthly Delights, a super sleazy bar beneath a flophouse near the corner of 18th and Mississippi in Potrero Hill. Another was the Frisco Club, on 6th Street, near Mission. We did a residency there, but the clientele was mostly drunks, street

Plimsouls, Troubadour, Los Angeles, 1979.

people, and just a few rock 'n' rollers of any description. Minnie's Can-Do Club, in the Fillmore, was predominately a jazz club where countercultural literati like Ruth Weiss once hosted a poetry series. It was a cool scene, and we played there, but our music seemed out of place there.

"The future punk people were hiding out in different scenes around the town. The street scene around Polk Street centered around the Haven, an all-night restaurant that let people hang out. This was where the glam scene met the gay street scene and the drug world. It was all happening, late night, at the Haven. We rehearsed right up the street from there. I lived in a residence hotel around the corner. Alejandro Escovedo was hanging around this scene at the time, though I didn't meet him until 1977 at Mabuhay Gardens, when the Nerves and Nuns were playing back-to-back nights. A lot of people I'd see later in bands in audiences in S.F. were from this scene."

It was a dizzying time that was literally morphing and changing underfoot.

"I had been playing on the street in San Francisco for about two years. The whole period of playing on the street was very exciting because it was almost the last gasp of the 1960s. Patti Smith has referred to 1974 as a huge energy year, and it was. There was an explosion in the folk clubs and poetry places. During 1973–74, I was on the streetcorner every night, from about 9 p.m. to 3 a.m. on Broadway and Columbus, right across from City Lights Bookstore. There was this other guy involved too, this guitar player from Alaska, who came down to California to meet up with Jack Lee. His name was Pat Stengl. Those guys are both from the same little town called Sitka, Alaska. They didn't come together, but they both came to San Francisco in the early seventies. So, Pat Stengl was in the Nerves, too, and he was playing lead guitar. We used to play with these little amps that were called Matthews Freedom Amps, and they took like fifty batteries, and they were really loud.

"The original concept was that we were going to write these songs and play them on the street and be the first band that blew up right off the street. We were going to do what the Beatles did, but our Hamburg strip bar was going to be the street. We were fashioning a whole new approach to music: loud and fast. Jack was a prolific writer. I was a performer and had written some of the lyrics. During my time on the street, I was re-creating myself and learning a lot about music and life. I was low man on the totem pole, driving the car, when we got one, and playing rhythm guitar.... He had a mad vision and was kind of on the run, and Paul Collins was not even in the picture yet. We were going to use amps that had batteries and rock right on the street, go to jail, and get really famous. But the problem was that the streets dried up after the winter of 1974. The energy dissipated over that winter and never came back. That vibe was gone, and we entered into a period of attrition and went into the clubs. It was like, 'Where is my generation?'"

Others were out there—dissidents and the discontent, the feverish and the focused, the art marauders and the agitators for the new.

"The psychedelic, outrageously dynamic theater group the Cockettes were still around S.F. at this time, and they were probably an influence on punk, especially Tomata du Plenty, who founded the Screamers down in LA. The Nerves wanted new music for our generation, minimal, just stripped of all the bullshit rock was loading onto everything. We hated guitar solos, the music business, radio, phony rock fans, standard rock clothes, long hair, and a lot of other things. And our music was very teenage-oriented, though I didn't really realize how much at the time.

"When the Nerves started up, there were no bands in San Francisco. There was Crime, and that was it. There were no Nuns, no Readymades, there was no any of that. No Sleepers. You'd see them around town, in North Beach. I knew those people by sight. But there was no movement yet. We did a residency on 6th Street, which went on and on. People didn't come to it. I don't think anybody knew we were there. The audience was mostly complete outlaws. There was no punk rock movement. One night the Meters came in. They must have been down on 6th Street for some reason. They were in town with the Stones. We did this residency on 6th Street, right up between Mission and Market. A few people came . . ."

That slender slice of time became an emboldening beacon, orienting people toward new possibilities, much of it raw and back-to-basics, rooted in the notion that music had stagnated, usurped by stadium rock performers gesturing in the hammiest way possible to faceless crowds.

"And then slowly it started, and by the time we came back up in April, there was a scene at Mabuhay just kicking off. It was born right between December and May. The first time we got on the radio, they weren't playing any other local bands. The Nerves got on the radio, I think it was New Year's Eve, 1976/1977. None of these groups seemed to be around, but the first band we crossed paths with was Crime, who were really ragamuffins. When we moved down to LA, we put on the first punk rock shows there with the Weirdos, Dils, Zeros, and the Germs. We had seven hundred bucks to our name and rented halls and invited everyone to play. But we left town to go on a national tour, the first by an unsigned independent band, as far as I know. We were gone for months and met the fledgling punk rock and new wave scene.

Every town had one or two bands playing original music. This was before the boom. We met Mink DeVille, Devo, Pere Ubu, and Suicide Commandos. The tour wrapped up with four nights at Max's Kansas City in NYC. At one point, we became the opening act for the Ramones for a number of shows on their *Rocket to Russia* tour.

"The whole period with the Nerves was like being in the Merchant Marines for me, like going around from city to city meeting people in the bands and audiences. It was very exciting. Yet, I still have never felt like I've been a part of any of the waves that have gone out. It hasn't been my experience, for some reason. Perhaps because of my restlessness, which pulls me out of things before things pop. I was always looking for something new.

"The Nerves broke up, and I was painting houses all throughout 1978. I was writing songs and trying to get together a band. On the very first day of 1979, I met this guy, Lou Ramirez, who had a nightclub gig in El Monte, California, a country-rockabilly-rock 'n' roll kind of five-sets-a-night, five-nights-a-week gig. He drafted me into that. The bass player and the drummer of that band ended up being in the Plimsouls, so we just started playing out there. I finally got fired from that gig. The boss said, 'Pete's on acid, he's fired.' So we started playing the nightclubs in Hollywood."

In the 1980s, as singer and guitarist, Case steered the Plimsouls, who became a much-lauded act, through their grass-roots Americana rich with melodies and tight Memphis rock 'n' roll sway. They made some inroads into the heartland's FM waves with tunes that defied "mythical surgary versions" of power pop by acts like 20/20; in doing so, the Plimsouls found the perfect "beat and melody" and retained "their broad vocabulary" as well as a "spine-tingling sense of urgency" (Young 47), even as they explored their own roots via covers of Mouse and the Traps and the Equals.

But another sense of roots was knocking on their door too.

"Tito from the Plugz was singing traditional Mexican songs singing in Spanish. He opened for people playing acoustic starting in the early 1980s. When the record company bought the Plimsouls equipment, I snuck in an acoustic guitar. We never owned any amps or equipment. We borrowed everything until we got signed. If you look at pictures, I am always on different guitars. When we got signed, they gave us some money to go down and buy stuff, and everybody got some Marshalls. I saw this Gibson Hummingbird, it was the first good acoustic guitar I had, and I just started playing that all the time at home. It got me back into the folk musicianship that I had experienced—country blues, Bob Dylan, and Lead Belly—the music I had grown up on."

The Plimsouls, Joseph's Foodliner, San Antonio, TX.

The Return of

The Plimsouls

From L.A. to S.A.

PLUS
SPECIAL GUEST
"INCOGNITO"

THIS SATURDAY

PROUDLY PRESENTED BY

Joseph's Foodliner & BEEHIVE UNLIMITED

AUG. 18

Joseph's Foodliner 2410 N. St. Mary's 734-2077

What happened post-gig sometimes became even more interesting and valued than the gigs themselves.

"In Lubbock, during the 1981 Plimsouls tour, I just suddenly woke up and said, 'I can't keep on doing this. I've got to take it to another place.' It was just a command. I started doing a jug band with the Plimsouls roadies, after the gigs in the hotel rooms, and it soon became more important to me than the gigs themselves. It was crazy, but that's what was happening.

"When you listen to those recordings from the Plimsouls tour in 1981, my roots are coming out, I am playing Jimmy Reed, which got documented on the live album *One Night in America*. We do Marvin Gaye's 'One More Heartache,' but we do it like a Howlin' Wolf song. Eddie played blues from Texas, Lou had a big influence from the East LA bands, and it was all there. The Nerves were almost like anti-roots. A lot of bands during 1977 were too. The Nerves music was very stripped down. It was a minimalist, compressed form of music, like the Ramones but different. Very song-oriented. When I was playing on the street in the seventies, I did a wide range of music. A typical set on the street would veer from Doc Pomus and 13th Floor Elevators to Lazy Lester. Jack wanted me in the band because he thought I could project rock 'n' roll music. But he really didn't understand what I was doing, and we'd argue about it."

After the Plimsouls, Case soon would become a traveling bard of intermingled folk traditions. Ever since, he has thrived as a keen-eyed troubadour that uses Bob Dylan–meets-beatnik wordplay to shed light on the nuances of relationships, landscapes, and the less-than-civic side of American life, like dire rent hikes, neglected military veterans, prisoners, small-town deaths, and overall struggles to survive.

"I think they call it roots because you need those roots to nurture the tree, nurture the musical form. The roots go down and feed everybody. I remember the first time I was hanging with Phil Alvin and I played 'Make Me a Pallet on Your Floor,' the Mississippi John Hurt version of that. We were riding around in the car, then sitting on a fence somewhere, playing the guitar, passing it back and forth and drinking quarts of beer. It was like '79. He was like, 'Wow, the Plimsouls have roots.' I guess it was news to him."

Case eventually would earn three Grammy nominations, including Best Traditional Folk Album in 2007 for *Let Us Now Praise Sleepy John*, confirming proof of his spirited originality, natural intellect, and ongoing vision. And each gig offered a glimpse into both his workaholic prowess—his ceaseless devotion to the hothouse of songs—and his churning moods, emotive wellspring, and poetic consistency.

The Plimsouls and the Blasters, California State University Long Beach Cafeteria, CA, 1979.

Peter Case, Mucky Duck, Houston, 2019, by David A. Ensminger.

"I grew up on the Beats, especially the work of Allen Ginsberg, Lawrence Ferlinghetti, and Jack Kerouac. They were very open about their selves and the process they used to write. So, I like that, but it's dangerous to speak too openly too often about songwriting; there are secrets that need to remain in the shadows. Where the real songs come from is a mystery. And just because you call it a song doesn't make it one. Songs communicate on a higher plane, and no one really knows how that happens. Songs still either come or they don't, but it's like a radio station on the air, and I'm pretty tuned into the channel when it's on. You gotta listen for the rustle a song makes as it approaches, and get in a place to get it down. There's things you learn to do. The original flash always has to be there or forget it."

While a music writer like me wants to ascribe some traits or methods in order to gather an understanding of how a tunesmith harnesses specificity versus vagueness, or carefully renders storytelling versus relying on empty pop fluff, Case rejects a "one size fits all" model: "Songs get authority from the subconscious. They don't have to be narrative, or anything else, but in a way, every song tells a story, just like every picture. The best, most powerful songs are indefinable, they just get you. There are no rules. There's an underground that uses blues, poetry, jazz, folk, the greatest country music, to tell the stories. America telling its own crazy story, looking for a way out of the maze . . .

"A sense of place is important to me, or was, but it's changed . . . the place is the place in your mind. Or imaginative, like a Shakespeare play set in Bohemia, but there's a seacoast that's not there in real life. I was obsessed with places, like New Orleans, Memphis, New York City, Buffalo, Dublin, Paris, Rome . . . Kathmandu, Timbuktu. But it's all changed now. I'm still in love and fascinated, but it's different."

Striking out on his own, Case was hungry for more adventure, not another slice of Americana with electric grit. His eponymous first solo album for Geffen became a harbinger of the Case to come. He offered up a nuanced world brimming with southern blues ("Ice Water" is a story set to the music of a Lightnin' Hopkins recording he learned), Irish traditionalism reinvented by post-punks (he covered the Pogues' "A Pair of Brown Eyes"), gripping narratives about people and places ("Small Town Spree" and "Satellite Beach"), and soaring melodies ("Echo Wars"). He earned a Grammy nomination for "Old Blue Car."

"T. Bone Burnett got the job because I picked him and persuaded the label. I liked working with him, and learned a lot, as he was *way* more experienced at recording than me. He's a good guy, crazy in a good way, not afraid to buck the powers a bit. 'Echo Wars' is cinematic music. My idea going into the record was to do 'folk' with a groove. By folk, I mean Scots-Irish, Appalachian, and blues strains. I was set on unraveling the mysteries of American music. I've been hollering about the decay of America for decades, on every record, but it is darker now. We've made some wrong turns as a society, and there's no going back . . . We're in a tough spot."

11

ALEJANDRO ESCOVEDO
A Man of Certain Influence

Born into a resplendent musical family that includes a brother, Javier, in the early punk stalwarts the Zeros and others who were lauded Latin jazz players, Alejandro Escovedo is a songwriting survivor who can weave together this country's current tumult with past ghosts like few others can. His 2018 album *The Crossing* explores characters caught in freeze-frame on America's wayward paths. Yet, much of the inspiration, as on many of his smart, infectious albums, stems from stories and history, lore and experience.

As mid-1980s stalwarts in Austin's frenetic clubs and bars, his band True Believers cemented his reputation as a rompin' rock 'n' roll guitar renegade. In the band, he was joined by his kin Javier Escovedo, who blazed at the slide guitar, and together they made a music that Vic Garbarini described in a nugget as "a stand-out among the recent crop of often overlooked . . . country punkers" that reminded him of the "Del Lords by way of Neil Young" (32). That spirit he still embodies on solo tunes like "Outlaw for You" and even more so on "Sonica USA," featuring lauded 1960's countercultural music visionary Wayne Kramer of MC5.

In the late 1970s, Escovedo helped ground the savvy rock 'n' roll of the Nuns, whose music seemed like lurid neon. As Gary Floyd noted in his memoir, watching them open for the Sex Pistols marked a rite of passage in his life. He was besotted. "Through the dank mist, I could see the Nuns were chewing through the last songs of their set. These people were great because they looked so severe and real, and sounded louder than bombs. I made a mental note to 'start band at once' and just stood there with my mouth open,

Alejandro Escovedo [left] with Richard Buckner, Rudyard's, Houston, TX, by Lana McBride.

watching the likes of skinny Alejandro Escovedo in his dire punk glory. Seeing the Nuns makes me special . . . right?"

It was a band marked deeply by the presence of Jennifer Miro, a striking blond figure influenced by Greta Garbo and Marlene Dietrich, who penned tunes with melodic, wooing vocals, including "Savage" and "Seduction Destruction." Escovedo was the band's early axe-man, who admired contemporaries like Pere Ubu, Avengers, and the Dils, but whose meaty chords and loose style delved back toward Pete Townshend of the Who and James Williamson of the Stooges but also the artier edge of Robert Fripp as well as the freedom of some jazz players.

Escovedo packed up and went east to New York City, then south to Austin. For years, the Texas state capital had been awash with both outlaw and cosmic country, and by the 1980s a rootsy counterculture had emerged out of the punk and new wave ashes and the revamped, revved-up rock 'n' roll traditionalism of bands like the Skunks and the Explosives, whose manner seemed invigorated but slightly wayward and feral. It was also the base of Joe "King" Carrasco, a favorite of Elvis Costello, whose intense regionalism and Tex-Mex music offered a "pervasive sense of humor and campily-phrased vocals" that characterized his "devotion to good-timin'," with the pumping Farfisa organ adding the necessary dash of Tabasco" ("Cuts"). From that scene—clubs as far afield as Raul's, Studio 29, Nightlife, Voltaire's, Club Foot, and many more—music became a restless character of many guises, each fielding fans in different ways.

There, Escovedo also helped steer dirt-stained Rank and File. As Tony Kinman recalled: "Al Escovedo had already bailed on the Nuns . . . because the music just wasn't interesting to him anymore. The notes were still going, but Al wasn't in them anymore ... A lot of the original bands were fading and petering out. I know in fact that the Avengers were on the verge of breaking, though I am not saying for the same reason I did, although it could be. I know that Penelope and Jimmy from the Avengers definitely went on to do something different than punk rock."

Adamantly vintage country in their rustic musings, like combining early Johnny Cash and Johnny Horton with a modern sly quirk, Rank and File became the epicenter of the burgeoning cowpunk genre and shook up Austin's new wave and indie scene.

Yet, part of Escovedo remains glued to the attitudes, style, and outlook he honed in his late 1970s excursion with the fiercely artful Nuns, one of the premier bands of punk's initial shockwave in seedy San Francisco. He readily explored that legacy on his album *Real Animal*, a breakthrough of sorts that led to live appearances with Bruce Springsteen, where together they unleashed the finely honed, warmly received pop-rock tune "Always a Friend," penned by Escovedo and Chuck Prophet.

The Crossing is a concept album, sometimes harkening back to *With These Hands*, his work from the mid-1990s that blurs fiction and autobiography by telling the tales of an America that is foreboding, troubled, and full of unfinished dreams. Though it takes creative turns, it is fully rooted in very gritty moments of Escovedo's edgy life.

Plus, it also waxes deeply poetic, as if in a Federico García Lorca frame of mind, about a sense of place. Whereas gay anti-fascist Lorca inspired tunes like "Spanish Bombs" by punk pioneers the Clash and penned poems that tackled Andalusia, Spain, which he described as full of "gypsies, horses, and archangels," or the Brooklyn Bridge, Escovedo continually peels back emotional layers relating to Texas.

In his own metaphoric lens, he scours the sun-punished borderlands, the nitty-gritty neighborhoods, the venal redneck bars. Each vicinity becomes a synecdoche of love and loathing, of belonging and fear. Texas is the marrow than runs through him, both life-giving and painful.

Many of his lyrics, including newer ones, are about broken fathers, troubled youth, bigots, and lawmen, as if he is exploring how men cope with their psyches, and other faulty, even dangerous, men in desperate times. And the result is stark powerful lines like "America is beautiful, America is ill ... America is a bloodstain in a honky tonk kill" found in the alluring tune "Teenage Luggage."

Other lyrics, like "Silver City," explore journeys fraught with possibility and peril. Throughout his catalog, he has plumbed his family's journey to America, his brash youthful journey through punk rock (the Nuns, time spent at Chelsea Hotel, Rank and File), and his harrowing journey through the aftermath of his wife's death and his hepatitis infection. Each such storyline becomes a ring of wood in his output, a layer of symbolism and searching. That it often crosses cultural histories, style, or territories doesn't appear to faze him, although realities on the street may still make him apprehensive.

"People are always amazed that there is this rock cross-cultural thing that happens, but in places like California, or even Austin, Chicanos play with white guys who play with Asian guys," he told me one night in Houston. "It seems pretty natural to me. But it's always been like that: look at the whole roots of rock and blues. I really don't get any of that shit from anybody inside music, but I do from people outside of it. I mean we go through shit when we tour, like down in the South. It was like a police state there when I played Hattiesburg, Mississippi, one time. Personally, I do have a sense of fear, and I don't feel comfortable."

Throughout his career, Escovedo has continually rebuilt his music and reinvented himself, finding a steady presence in being inventive but never forsaking his sense of a modern, dark serenade. Sometimes his albums are rich in production values, sometimes stripped to the bone, like the live work *More Miles Than Money*. Others rock to the hilt, like *A Man Under the Influence*, while some experiment in sound and vision, like *The Boxing Mirror*.

"What [someone like] Richard Buckner does and I do are two very different things, but we share something in terms of the music. The places where the music comes from is completely different because my music does come from a more traditional rock place. I can do a Roxy Music song, a John Cale song, a Stooges song. Then I can do a song like 'Broken Bottle' and a song about an arrhythmic castanets player, but Richard's music is different. What I love about Richard is that his lyrics are really beautiful, and his voice is very rich and deep. And that is a place where you wanna go, and that's where people rarely take you."

Altogether, his songs seem both offhand and meticulous, inked on the back of a hotel receipt or restaurant napkin, yet carved in careful lines under the moon too. They wax specific but also universal, stemming from eyewitness truths but bending the tales to find deeper impressions. Any Latino immigrant could be the kid facing a former Texas Ranger with yellow teeth and deep-down prejudice found in the spoken-word "Rio Navidad."

The Crossing tends to merge worlds, manners, and impressions. It feels like correspondence from an America bruised and roughened by injustice. Though his meditations seem lore-inducing or trancelike, they quickly strip mystery of its opaqueness. On "Footsteps in the Shadows," dark shapes dancing across the treeline during a storm's impending blitzkrieg actually indicate men with hounds chasing down people.

The tune is ominous and engrossing. The hunters know nothing of the lives they hound, batter, and terrify. It reveals the flipside of this country's history—its naked animosity towards the vulnerable and "other."

Much of the album works through an unsettling mishmash of burning cigarettes, honky-tonk jails, and shitty guitars. Escovedo does not skimp on details: he enters into the maps of a Latino emotional topography and brings a human touch to bear on the conflicts. Texas is not the Lone Star State of highly exaggerated largeness—pine thickets and expansive prairies, cattle ranches, big cars, and spurts of oil—it is a slice of Mexico removed by war and treaty. It is an old country, mythic, a mother.

That's what Escovedo explores with tuning-fork clairvoyance, just as he is able to find easygoing reference points—reels that spin with the contributions of Latinos to rock 'n' roll's underbelly. That is why he calls out the Zeros, punk originators from 1976 featuring his brother Javier Escovedo, in the lyrics of "Sonica USA." That band acted as a ballast, keeping music meaningful in an era of stadium rock mediocrity. With such gumption and respect, Escovedo documents how Latinos made music that pushed back against monolithic monoculture. They were wild seeds.

When Escovedo shouts out, he is not simply paying tribute or looking back with an earnest, hard-fought wink. The act is about revering, in a very tensile, tactile, and spirited way, the resilience of a counterculture often undergirded by Latinos. Since this may have gone unnoticed by many, even as punk legends like Alice Bag and El Vez (the alias of Robert Lopez of the Zeros) have spent years reclaiming such stories, Escovedo makes it a cornerstone on *The Crossing*.

In the end, Escovedo seems indifferent to the dodgy psychology of here-and-now Instagram memes and Twitter fake furor. He is far more invested in the steady gravity of truths distilled in songs and news that is always news. He tries to undo the dead weight of time. In the arc of his narratives, it does not matter if tragedy unfolded ten minutes ago or in a crinkled crevice of the past.

His tunes make the pain, the suffering, the hiding, the exodus, the mingling, and the living, all the bitter rides and hardened solace, as well as the joy, feel immediate, close to the skin, and undimmed.

12

MIKE WATT

Portrait of the Artist as a Bass Man

"Cowpunk seemed to be about gimmick schtick big label foist, but also it's about music just being music and punk being less a style than a state of mind you could bring to different kind of musical motifs," Mike Watt of Minutemen reminded me recently. "Of course, 'cow-punk' and 'hardcore' both share two-step beat lots of time—so does klezmer—so I can see music connect there. The first guy I heard use 'cowpunk' was that guy from the Surf Punks (get it?) who put it in part of his 'stage name'—Scott 'Cowpunk' Goddard. I 'pert-near wanna heave at that word but will admit it's not as bad as 'new wave,' 'alternative,' or 'grunge.' Shit like that really weirds me out. I can't handle it."

Minutemen remain a rare breed of punk themselves, endlessly weaving together blunt shards of funk, frenetic brief jazz leanings, slanted and enchanted throwbacks to rock 'n' roll, and spoken-word Beat poetics. But drawing the line between them and sources is not necessarily easy, for their sense of history may not be a matter of music alone.

As bass player for Minutemen, fIREHOSE, the reformed Stooges, and countless other projects, Watt is almost an indescribable force of punk nature, someone whose roots are deeply wedged in the south Los Angeles/San Pedro landscape.

His work continues to blend Jack Kerouac beat language kicks, John Coltrane soulful musical expansiveness, and port town humor, work ethic, and grit with equal aplomb and adaptability. He is not merely a survivor, though he did overcome a near-death medical ailment; he is a supercharged folk hero. "The illness was twenty years ago," Watt reminded me. "And I got my second

Mike Watt + The Missingmen, Pop Obscure Records, Los Angeles, 2018, by David A. Ensminger.

opera (*The Secondman's Middle Stand*) out of it. Also, it led to me playing with J. Mascis + The Fog, and probably the Stooges, I shit thee not. Life is trippy."

He is also a homespun style surrealist—listen to the uncanny music of his project Big Walnuts Yonder—plus an emblem of what remains true and tried, organic and productive in modern music. He upends all notions of music careerism, art as commodity, and literary journey making.

Even his 2016 album *"Ring Spiel" Tour '95*, is an incredible slice of tour documentation highlighting his superstar assemblage, including Pat Smear, Eddie Vedder, and Dave Grohl (whose drums are dizzying and acrobatic), that gathered for the twenty-three-gig trek through the cramped clubs of Bill Clinton–era underground America. It is a bygone moment, a convergence and nexus like few others, whose tunes like "Against the '70s" were caught on blistering tape in front of a rapt Midwest audience.

Watt's legacy seemed even more important in the reactionary political climate of the Trump era, including "Political Song for Michael Jackson to Sing," featured on the '95 live album. "I wrote it," tells Watt. "D. Boon wrote better tunes, but I wrote that one and sent it to Mike Jackson's management. I thought if he sang that tune, we never ever have to explain our band again. I never got an answer back."

Next page: Minutemen, on WKDU, Philadelphia, PA, 1984, by D. Boon.

the MINUTEMEN AND Red Scare

WKDU 91.7 FM

PLUS:
Constraint BETHLEHEM
AND **No Control** N.Y.

SAT. JULY 28th

PHILADELPHIA

CAMPAIGN TRAIL 84

LOOK FOR THE MINUTEMEN'S NEW DOUBLE-ALBUM "DOUBLE NICKELS ON THE DIME" ON SST RECORDS

And I wondered if the band's principles, ideas, or point of view expressed in the tune could be an important lens into the current uncertain era.

"I can't, in all fairness, pretend I can say what D. Boon would say, but . . . I wish to god I could hear him weigh in on all this. Your question is exactly how I feel. You can't know how much I miss him as a dear buddy but also as a voice thinking of the people and not just himself. I know Raymond [Pettibon] sure ain't into this [current political] crap, but then it's been around in other forms with other douches as well. I think of what D. Boon wrote once for that song 'Shit from an Old Notebook':

let the products sell themselves
fuck advertising, commercial psychology
psychological methods to sell should be destroyed

"By the way, that was the last Minutemen song I ever recorded using a pick on bass. It was all fingers after that."

Watt's gigs and efforts still contain a strong element of conscience, like aiding Doctors Without Borders, an organization helping the desperate in warzones and other places of calamity, mirroring the conscience of D. Boon.

"Yeah, I like that organization much, like their ethics about humans helping humans. It's a nightmare they have to deal with maximalist power trips, but they keep on keepin' on with somehow trying to preserve some kind of humanity between us."

But his sense of roots has many sides and shapes. For one, he is a person who has webs of experiences branching off in a thousand territories.

"Every stitch I find myself in I try to make a place to learn and to get further down the road with bass and composing. I think of life as one big classroom, and folks I come in contact with are most kind when they share what makes them *them* with me. I believe everyone has something to teach me—that could mean a kid just starting on bass. It's what I was trying to say with my third opera, *Hyphenated-Man*: life is for learning. I'll tell you this about Iggy, for sure the 125 months I served with the Stooges had him making me a way better bass player . . .

"Also, Thurston Moore helped me big time after D. Boon got killed. He was the one that got me on bass again after that wreck. I owe everyone so much, like the guys I play with now. It never quits, and in my mind, why should it? Being on bass, you really learn to work with people cuz working bass can be like being like glue: with nothing to stick to, you're just a puddle. Sometimes

Minutemen, The International Club, Houston, TX.

you give direction (my operas), sometimes you take direction (Porno for Pyros, J. Mascis, Stooges) and sometimes you collaborate (CUZ, Il Sogno Del Marinaio, Big Walnuts Yonder). For me, it's like inhale/exhale . . ."

But what seems to bug Watt is how people set up guardrails for music and then police them: "I don't like the idea of genre—music is music for me and segregation thinking seems to me is promoted by putting labels on styles of how people work their bands and their sounds. The movement really opened up my mind like a sledgehammer to the Berlin walls in my head telling me what music was what before I even fucking heard it. On my *Watt from Pedro* show, I struggle with people who can't talk about their music stuff without referencing other music stuff, like what the fuck—is this junior high? For me, that kind of shit starts to remove this kind of expression from the realm of what music is for me."

Sometimes "roots" means plumbing through the past, rich in anecdotes, childhood reminiscing, and family flashbacks, all of which can as much give shape to a person as musical immersion and bombardment.

"Hearing my pop's tour stories (he did Vietnam tours in the engine room) sure as hell got me curious about wanting to see what he was telling me

beyond baroque presents

THE MINUTEMEN

LAWNDALE

plus special guest evangelist

BROTHER AWEST
WORLD SALIVATION MINISTRY

Saturday, April 6, '85, starting at 9 pm
Beyond Baroque
681 Venice Boulevard, Old Venice City Hall
Venice, (213) 822-3006
NO AGE LIMIT

about . . . the first couple days back from tour he'd take me driving for hours and hours with him spieling about what he saw in the last nine months or whatever—I was fucking hanging on every word! It really made me curious about the world. I think for sure that was my big motivation into being INTO touring and NOT against it. D. Boon liked the adventure part of it too. His pop was only in the Navy four years (radio man) but maybe that got into him also."

Like many punks, that background shaped a sense of life often outside the norms: "My background with Navy housing definitely had me living with all kinds of different people—well, only enlisted men and no officers, in my case, but as far as ethnic background, I was with all kinds of people and I know that shaped me big time. These two things had *huge* effects on me later in my life. Maybe work ethic too . . .

"I remember my pop once telling me 'you know you're gonna have to pull some regular duty too' after hearing about some music stuff. He didn't realize I was doing music for a living 'til I started sending him postcards from tour a few years before cancer took him in 1991. He was only fifty-one, and it killed him in nine months. It was a really brutal cancer death, thank god only nine months. It was very hard on me."

That legacy of his father left him with deep impressions, often in unexpected ways.

"My pop did some teaching when he had shore duty—this from a guy who never graduated high school. He taught nuke engine stuff. After he retired, though, he did something he learned in the Navy right when he got in at eighteen (actually joined the guard at seventeen): refrigeration repair. And he retired to Clovis, just north of Fresno—where there's no ocean! Tells you something about the Navy . . ."

Whether the Pedro region affected him as a writer is to be debated, or as Watt states: "I've written about Pedro in my songs, but I'm not from here. I came here when I was nine from Virginia, but does that matter? Maybe . . . I wrote 'Song for Dave Alvin' for the person, not much about California though he's from Downey, I think, or at least part. Sly Stone said, 'it's not where you're from, it's where you're at,' and I think he did cuz you can't pick where you're from, but maybe you have a little choice (hopefully) where you wanna be."

When I tried to unlock Minutemen lyrics, attempting to find San Pedro allusions, shoreline metaphors for the sea and tide shifts, ropes, and anchors, Watt's input went another direction: "'Themselves' was written by D. Boon, and I know it was inspired by the CCR song 'Don't Look Now' cuz he told me.

Minutemen, Santa Monica Civic, CA, 1981.

Mike Watt, Minutemen, by Edward Colver.

Previous page: Minutemen, Santa Monica Civic, CA.

We covered that tune but not a straight copy: our version imagined Curtis Mayfield playing cuz we were really into *Curtis/Live!* at the time . . . Dez from Black Flag turned us on to the album. Minutemen covered Creedence Clearwater Revival and Blue Oyster Cult cuz that's where we learned how to play, copying their tunes. When I met D. Boon, we were twelve, and Creedence was the only rock band he knew! Our first gig we went to was T. Rex. We actually did cover T. Rex now that I remember: 'Prelude,' which was an instrumental off of their *Beard of Stars* album.

"'The Anchor' words were from George Hurley, and he told us it was about him having a dream where he was Mick Jagger, kind of. He always let me title his tunes, and I used the refrain for that one. I wrote 'Beacon . . .' and 'Mutiny . . .' words, 'Brave Captain' from some *Lifeboat* kind of movie. Reverend Jim Jones informed 'Mutiny . . .' and 'Beacon . . .' had some connect with mota [weed]. 'Dr. Wu' is a Steely Dan cover that I had nothing to do with. 'Plight' words were from D. Boon. What's trippy about the album and the tunes on *What Makes a Man Start Fires?* is that it's the only Minutemen album where

I wrote all the music. I wrote half the words, but all the music cuz I was at home having two major knee surgeries, one right after the other, and there was a lot of both hurting and laying on the deck."

When I discovered Mike Watt's thrill of listening to Ornette Coleman in the early 1980s, I partly assumed that it influenced Watt's unique sense of song composition, but, as Watt noted to me, the truth is: "*Dancing in Your Head* was first Ornette Coleman I really got into. Joe Baiza [Saccharine Trust] hipping to me to Ornette was big time. I ended up meeting the man for a few moments. He was great cat. I saw him live with his son Denardo with Prime Time. I was with Pettibon (artist, zinester) and loved it. One of the bassmen—there was two of everything in this band. One of 'em, Jamaaladeen Tacuma, broke a string in the first number and kept charging hard the whole gig with just three left!"

That persistence and unfazed stamina almost seems the most powerful impression of all, except that Coltrane made an even more penetrating impact, for it, and the companionship of Pettibon, seemed to open new routes, pathways, and roots.

"Even way more important was Raymond Pettibon turning me on to John Coltrane.

"'Ascension' was the first thing he played for me (I thought he was an older punk rocker!) and he took me to gigs to see, in person, Elvin Jones, Mr. Ray Brown, Max Roach, Cecil McBee, Sam Rivers, Yma Sumac, Little Jimmy Scott, blind Al Hibbler, Tad Farlow, Albert 'Tootie' Heath, Warne Marsh, Teddy Edwards, Horace Tapscott, Kenny Burrell, and fucking buttloads of those older cats still gigging. So fucking inspirational for me, truly."

Benefit for Indian Fishing Rights, with Minutemen, Cathay de Grande, Los Angeles.

13

THE HICKOIDS
Harness the Corn Demon

The mid-1980s also witnessed the rise of inveterate cowpunks the Hickoids. For four dizzying decades, they have been the cream of the crop of Texas musical rowdiness by stirring up hootenannies, take-no-prisoners satire, mutant twang, and subverted Southern rock 'n' roll. Jeff Smith leads them into these crazed forays and steers the Hickoids to invoke their own genre, "corn-punk," because they fit no categories nor do they feign to fit any trends. They are singular unwashed figures in the music "business," and they always seek a special brand of mayhem. The choice of covers on their 2011 album *Kicking It with the Twits* tells a tale. The bluesy, laid-back harmonica hollering of "Pictures of Lily" yanks the Mod hipness of the Who out from underneath Pete Townshend's shaggy hairdo and injects whiskey-breath swaggers that wallow in stupor and stomp. It's careening, not calculated, and charged-up as any San Antonio roadhouse could muster. In more up-tempo flair, they tackle "Have You Seen Your Mother, Baby, Standing in the Shadow?" with organ bliss-outs and slapdash honky-tonk, kickin' around the Mick Jagger territory with fine form, singlehandedly making the dusty 45 record feel reanimated in their greasy hands.

Hickoids pump tunes with plenty of rough aplomb to slay slack-jawed boredom, especially in the digital era of plastic perfection. Without flinching, they can also effortlessly inject a dirty slab of bubblegum rock style borrowed from the likes of Slade, thus rollick and roll close to the bone of the original year of '73. Raising howls in this newfangled world of redux new wave, fake soul music, and overwrought cheesy pop, they carry on, regardless, like sexed-up soldiers of the dank Lone Star night.

Jeff Smith, Cactus Music, Houston, TX, 2019, by David A. Ensminger.

"The band was really conceived as hardcore country meets hardcore punk," says singer Jeff Smith. "When Jukebox—the original Hickoids guitarist whose signature sound, a mid-1960's Mustang played through a Fender amp with heavy use of the 'whammy' bar that marks our debut album and *Hard Corn*—and I first started working on tunes for the band, I don't think either of us had much idea what the end result was going to sound like. Jukebox was a lot more earnest about the country part of the equation in the beginning. To him, it was more about injecting psychedelia into the country (think Jimi Hendrix, not the Byrds) and still bringing the punk energy, which I think we did pretty well on songs like 'O.A.F. Anthem' and 'It's a Beautiful Thang.'" Either way, the music meant blowing up genre boundaries, and making them much more elastic and convergent, all linked to DIY traditions underscored by satire—nothing done without a wink.

To anyone who actually believes in the cardboard box of genres, albums like *We're In It For The Corn* and the EP *Hard Corn* (seemingly a pun on both hardcore and hard porn) are a sputtering papier mâché volcano of roots punk transgression possibilities that recalls the not-so-salad days of Texas-bred, dirt pie surrealism and subversion, from Scratch Acid and Cargo Cult to Stickmen with Rayguns and Culturcide. It amounted to a homebrewed hootenanny

Hickoids, The Axiom, Houston, TX.

of doctored and demented music I like to term "acid-billy," like a Nick Cave version of *Hee-Haw* (whose theme they raucously cover).

Somehow, in the midst of the Reagan era of trickle-down economics and the Iran-Contra scandal, the band predated and served as a premonition for the likes of Rev. Horton Heat, Southern Culture on the Skids, the Cows, and others, but with a more intense, lunatic fringe. It was dubbed corncore since hardcore had become formularized and recycled endlessly, more belted down and boilerplate every time. Instead of this shuttered vision, Hickoids offer a countrifried pandemonium fueled by speed demons, a country jester's version of Antonin Artaud's Theatre of Cruelty, and snake-charming southern-preacher front-porch babel/babble. It's a smorgasbord of styles that funnels true country restlessness, taking Jason and the Scorchers into a wired, warped, and wily cannibalized form of roots music, including the frantic and frenetic "Animal Husbandry," which bursts across earlobes like a nickel-fed plastic pony in the parking lot of Walmart gone berserk.

In tidy liner notes, Ken Lieck does an uncanny job of describing all this as "saw-toothed rock...drawled lyrics...and cauterized chicken scratch guitar riffs" purged of everything but sheer Texas-sized gusto. Even instrumentals like "Rodeo Peligroso" feel part sci-fi, part bratwurst, part LSD. Meanwhile,

"Williamanza" reeks of sea shanties and the theme of *Rawhide*, all thrusts and totemic power, resembling a hillbilly Adam and the Ants fueled by cases of Pearl beer. "Hickoid Heaven" could be a scruffy, hill-country, hen-scratching Pogues, whereas "The Longest Mile," though atomized, is a little more cookie cutter in style, in contrast to their Elvis explosion of "Burning Heart of Love" or their "Corn Foo Fighting," in which they pillage the classic funk-schlock of Carl Douglass. The 1970s never seemed so . . . unbridled. This is truly one of those thermometers that measures the roaring ruckus of an age when punk was far more than a few historic sidenotes or nostalgia in waiting. This was the age of trampling insurrection, bleary boisterousness, and gut-wrenching gumption.

"I wrote the music for a few of the early songs, but I was and still am very limited on the guitar," admits Smith. "And, to me, it was always more about the humor . . . we knew we could piss off the rednecks before we ever got started but over time it became funny to see how humorless the punks could be, especially as hardcore eclipsed punk. But Jukebox felt that we were destined to be some sort of mainstream rock 'n' roll sensation even though he was a really fucking funny and smart guy. On some level, he lacked a little self-awareness about our place in things at that time. After he left the band, we recorded *Walt-a-Cross-Dress Texas*, which he referred to as "the gay album."

Roots punk had become the de rigueur trend by the mid-1980s in Austin, from Rank and File and the True Believers to the Wild Seeds and even the gruff garage rock of Poison 13, to a lesser degree. But Hickoids, like the Ideals, seemed like an alternative to roots music as well as hardcore, though they harnessed hardcore's hectic speed in tunes like "The Longest Mile."

"Historically, it's a little difficult to explain," says Smith, "but, by some standard punk musicians were not considered musicians at all with a lot of folks clinging to the notion they had when the Ramones and Sex Pistols first came out. We drank at the same bars, knew the same drug dealers, and chased a lot of the same girls, but because we weren't 'working musicians,' and indeed had skipped a lot of the journeyman steps, we were considered lesser. And I think bands like X and the Blasters, in spite of their poetry and artistry, suffered the same stigma in LA. But of course, in LA it was about selling records, and nobody really cared about anything else if you could do that—you'd have fifty bands trying to cop your look and sound within a week if you scored a top ten out there.

"It wasn't really our desire to do anything mainstream (in spite of my comment regarding Jukebox above) or 'pop sounding.' For us, the Eagles were just as lowly as Kenny Rogers. True Believers, Wild Seeds, the Offenders, and

Hickoids, Continental Club, Austin, TX.

the Dicks were all friends and great bands, but I guess I will just say we were trying to create our own 'bag' and would take whatever we wanted from either shopping cart." They were the true motley crew.

But one notable change was taking place in cowpunk and roots punk. Women, who had participated in punk in droves, were also deeply involved—Tex and the Horseheads, Blood on the Saddle, and Lone Justice. "It's absolutely true," Smith agrees. "Historically, country music always had a strong female presence among the performers and the same held true with cowpunk. I saw a good couple of hundred 'hardcore' bands in the last half of the eighties and I bet I didn't see ten women on stage. And as Davy Jones noted, hardcore just lacked sex, outside of the somewhat homoerotic ritual of shirtless young men banging into and touching each other."

Mike Watt contextualizes it slightly differently: "'Hollywood punk,' 1970s stuff, had lots of women, proportionately, but 'hardcore' is when it changed. I guess some of this 'roots stuff' you're talking about tried to bring back the ladies, but it was still never the same. Annette from Blood in the Saddle was the bass player in the Bangs before Bangs would change their name to the Bangles and got a new bass player. D. Boon made the Blood on the Saddle album happen for New Alliance Records. He saw them play and asked them to be on the label. They did their own recording and artwork." So, not only did women make an imprint on punk, spanning from first wave to the roots rock uprising, the DIY ethos remained consistent between the two eras as well.

Still, it was a period very different from the 1990s, when alt-country Uncle Tupelo and Whiskeytown garnered praise from the likes of *No Depression* while the grunge-punk phenomenon was pumped tirelessly by mainstream media. "Well, I've often said that the only thing being first at something guarantees you is that you'll die drunk, alone, and broke," admits Smith. "Luckily, I'm none of those things, but I don't owe much of it to music either. Well, that's not true, just being snarky. Most of my lifelong friends are folks I met playing music in the 1980s. Seriously, I guess the analogy I would use is that we (Hickoids and our contemporaries) were the gateway drug that was still in the testing stage and probably not suitable for wide consumption."

Alarmingly, some icons are being diminished, forgotten, or erased. Smith observes: "Hell, most people barely even know who Doug Sahm is outside of San Antonio, Austin, and 'music snob' circles, and he almost singlehandedly invented what is known as 'Americana.'" But while *No Depression* swept the land, bands like Hickoids, never quite fitting the mold of expectations, grew more obscure. "I guess the real answer is simply that we were ahead of our

Jeff Smith, Under the Volcano, Houston, TX, 2021, by David A. Ensminger.

time, and I choose to remain frozen there, at least ideologically. Nirvana wasn't the greatest punk band in the world. David Geffen needed a new way to market blue jeans or whatever and Kurt Cobain was his answer. The popularity of the other bands [like Uncle Tupelo, then Son Volt and Wilco] was the culmination of a lot of things that happened culturally and in the media. I'll just say they had a sturdier platform to stand on."

14

THE BEATNIGS

When You Wake Up in the Morning

For people tuned into late 1980s San Francisco punk, the Beatnigs carried forward the promise of hybrid experimentation, a stout unwavering political ethos, uncanny finesse, and artful adventure. Signed to the legendary punk record label Alternative Tentacles, their smoldering tune "Television, The Drug Of The Nation" unleashed in 1988 became a calling card of their musical prowess and intelligence. It revealed their ability to deconstruct media, attack the powers-that-be in the Reagan-Bush era, and form a trenchant groove at the same time. By utilizing industrialized punk-hiphop and atavistic performance art to sharpen their message, they seemed cutting edge but also avidly old school too, partly due to singer Michael Franti's (Disposable Heroes of Hiphoprisy, Spearhead) penetrating tone, wry wordplay, and pulsating elocution. That side evoked both sociopolitical fervor and musical prowess.

Nimble drummer Kevin Carnes held down the rhythm section of the Beatnigs with elastic aplomb. But prior to joining their efforts he played with the Usuals, alongside Adam Sherburne, in Houston. The Usuals gigged at clubs like the Omni, and Sherburne later helped shape the sonic smarts of left-wing savvy Consolidated, whom Carnes joined briefly. Since those early years, Carnes has continued to pump his vigor, skill, and spirit into an array of projects, including: Soulstice, Parliament-Funkadelic, Eric McFadden Trio, Electrofunkadelia, Storm Inc. and IZM.

For Carnes, who has called the band Afro-punk and Black Militant, "Beatnigs name alone was tough to swallow, add the way we dressed, wore our hair, and behaved in public. I've had Black elders come to me and tell me how they hated our name but once they heard and saw us perform it made sense to them

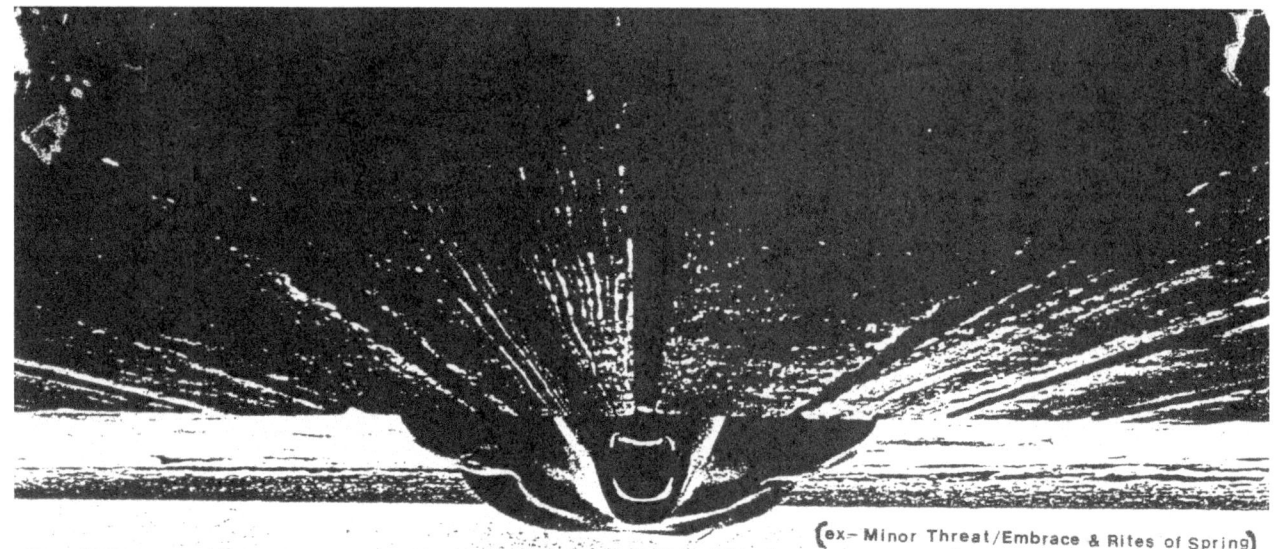

BEATNIGS (ex- Minor Threat/Embrace & Rites of Spring)
FUGAZI

CRIMPSHRINE   YEASTIE GIRLZ

GILMAN ST PROJECT
924 gilman st berkeley
Friday May 20   9pm

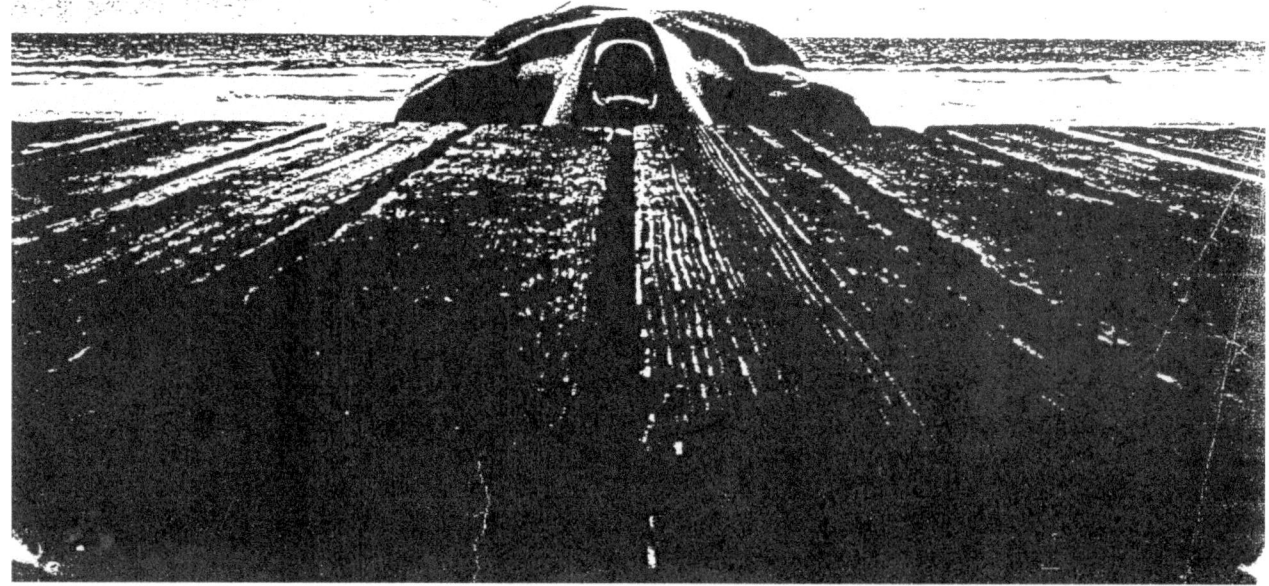

and they loved us for what we were doing, and they *still* didn't like the name. The name, the music, the words, the performance it was all meant to challenge whoever was standing in front of us. Being that we were playing at a lot of punk clubs and art bars, most of the people there were white and I'm sure some people took what we were giving in a negative way and others understood the unconditional love that was ever present at our shows. I'll remind you that it was also a play on the Beat Generation—we were exactly that."

At first listening, the Beatnigs seem to meld the world of Gil Scott-Heron and the Last Poets with industrial rock a la Wax Trax records, plus the political-mindedness of Fugazi and Dead Kennedys; but as Carnes reminded, their influences were wide and supple.

"There was a lot of music shared between the members of the band, everything from Public Enemy to Bad Brains, The Art Ensemble of Chicago and Sun Ra. On the industrial side of things, there was a group called Test Department from England and another Bay Area crew called Survival Research Laboratories that were the biggest influences on us. West African music, particularly percussion-oriented stuff, seemed to always be playing in the background. I was a DJ during that time. Some of us were really into fashion and visual arts and technology, while others were doing carpentry. Many of us rode bicycles as our main mode of transportation. We smoked and drank and talked into the wee hours like the bohemians we were. It's all there in the music."

While other members of Beatnigs came from California and Hong Kong, Carnes grew up in Detroit, which has a long tradition of radical rock 'n' roll and counterculture funk, from MC5 to Funkadelic, including mastermind George Clinton, with whom Carnes worked with on projects too. Carnes seemed to soak up Detroit music and perspectives.

"Yeah, the 'edge,' the industrial Midwest, the Motor City, Motown, the beautiful contrast of spring and fall and *slush*! It's all here in spirit," says Carnes. "Someone recently asked if I still have kinship with that place, and without hesitation I said yes. I love it there and hope for its recovery.

"First off, I learned a lot more than just dynamics from George Clinton, and I have to mention Blackbyrd McKnight and Lige Curry as two others from that circle of musicians that helped me grow as musician, drummer, and performer. They are all top-shelf human beings.

"Bernie Worrell is another one. A master at his craft yet fully in the moment with whomever is on the stage. He makes playing music fun, and if you're paying attention he'll say some funny shit right in the middle of rockin' the most ridiculous solo or comping behind someone else's idea. Classical

Beatnigs, Gilman St. Project, Berkeley, CA.

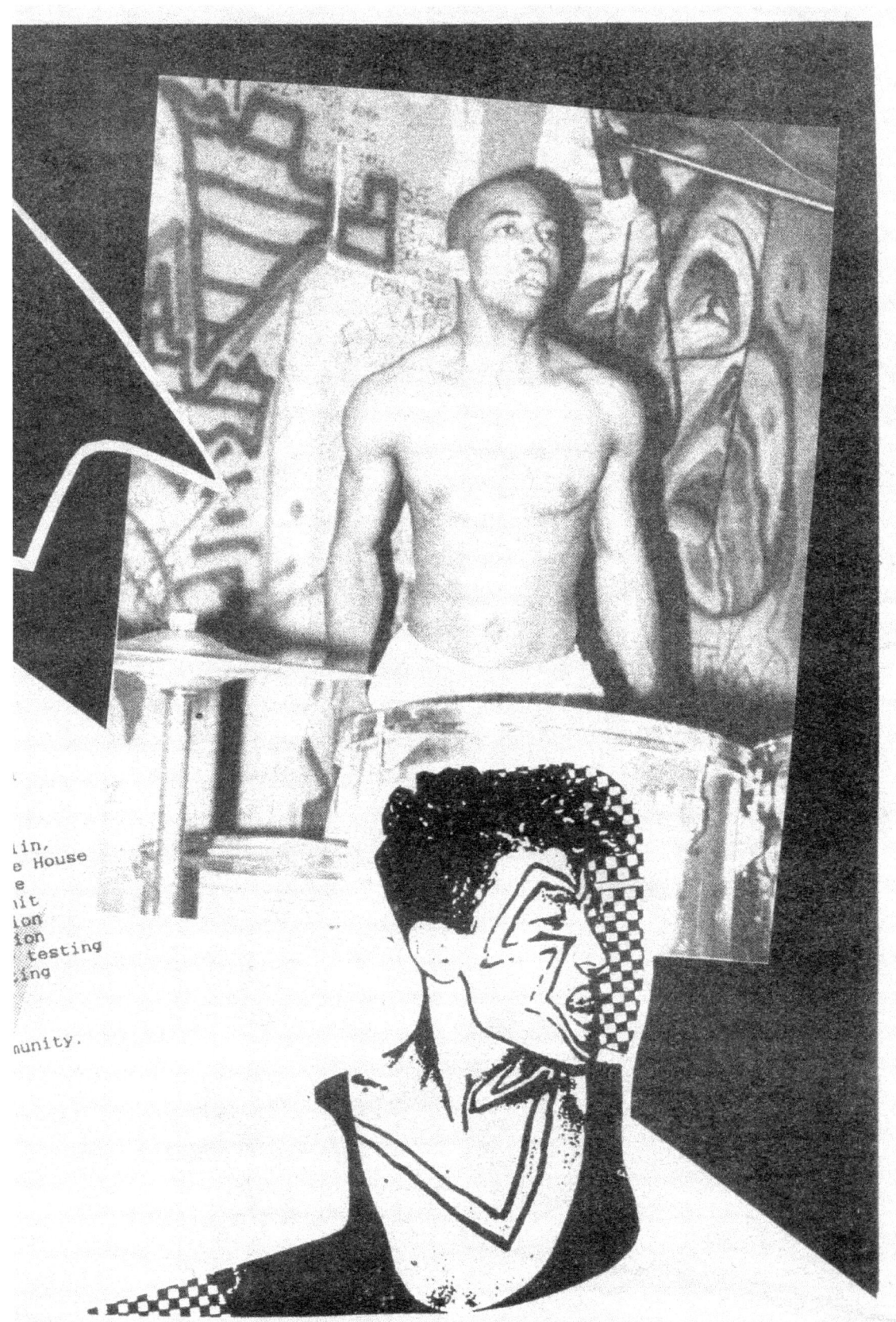

references followed by cartoon theme songs all sprinkled with gospel, jazz, and the funk, and all within a single passage of music. I was already a good listener, but being present with yourself and the people you're playing with and having a sense of humor? He just took me to another level of awareness. He didn't so much teach me things as much as confirm them for me."

As singer Michael Franti once told *Maximum Rocknroll*, the Beatnigs live show was partially catalyzed by a desire to be different from the hordes of MTV mediocrity and return to "got-to-be-there," highly vivid live performances. Carnes continues: "It was much harder to capture the cacophony and girth of the band on tape than to bring the studio ideas to the stage. From the beginning, rehearsals were like being in the studio, sometimes music studio, sometimes dance studio, and other times art studio. That's just how we started out working: taping jams, making samples, and building songs from them, finding something to do with a gas tank, a string of Christmas lights, and a circular saw. Up until the release of our record, there were never two Beatnigs shows that were the same. The agenda, themes, story lines, and gear were constantly changing, evolving, and that's how we liked it. We didn't start out as a band in the conventional sense, though we became one. I have always performed as if it may never happen again and all of my favorite bands, the Usuals, the Beatnigs, and the Broun Fellinis embodied a need to stir the pot of human existence."

And true to their forefathers in pointed and polemical Black music history, the tunes like "Rootigus Sporaticus" lashed out against nuclear testing and interventionism, while songs like "Burrito" offered blatant humor even while observing issues about class and race.

"Global politics can't exist without personal politics, and I've never thought 'Burritos' was funny, though it is very clever," Carnes insists. "Everything we talked about on stage we lived, and however many years later class and race are still two of the biggest social problems in this country. It was very important to us to talk about what was right underfoot and what we were experiencing on the daily right here in the Bay, which many folk like to say is so 'free' and 'liberal,' but the reality for some? Not so much.

"We played with MDC, Fugazi, Living Colour, the Butthole Surfers, and Schooly D. We jammed with Genesis P-Orridge and Einsturzende Neubauten as well as countless fans that were brought up on stage or had the stage dumped on them. Don't remember a show with D.O.A. Don't be mad, I stayed pretty high back then. We did lots of benefits throughout our career. I feel like it's the duty of all artists and entertainers. I learned that from Adam

The Beatnigs, *Maximum Rocknroll*, No. 56, January 1988.

Sherburne of the Usuals and Consolidated, and to this day, I continue to share my musical talents to help bring attention and funding to others."

Meanwhile, songs like "Television" examined the role of the government, mass media, and public apathy with aplomb, yet mass media has now metastasized from five big corporate stations to endless outlets across various platforms, including endlessly streaming on handheld devices.

"I can't speak for Michael, who wrote the lyrics, but yes," Carnes acknowledges, "I personally feel like the (mis) 'information age' is both wondrous and wretched, and I'm really glad that I'm not a young person trying to get my footing in so much (m)ass media trash."

Many people may know his work across the punk, industrial, and jazz spectrum, but Carnes also drummed on rousing renditions of "The Great Leap Forward" by socialist urban singer-songwriter Billy Bragg, when Beatnigs joined him and Michelle Shocked for a 1988 tour.

"It was unexpected. Billy Bragg was doing 1,000–2,500 seaters at that time and most of those shows were near sellouts. We were an unexpected treat for most of the folks that were going to that show. As was Michelle Shocked. She was still very new to the world at that time. So, if you're going out to hear one politico artist, getting three different performances on the same stage? The fact that we sounded nothing alike was a moot point from the first note. Then when it got around that the fire marshal was showing up at each venue to make sure we weren't going to burn the place down, it was over with. Folks had to be there."

15

X

Under the Big Black Moon

With his rich baritone quiver and chiseled looks, John Doe has been an uber-indie songwriter who survived the swells of his bands X and Knitters while honing a singular style all his own. As co-helmsman and titanic presence in X, he became a gutsy and savvy songster effortlessly channeling countercultural references in the ragged glory years of LA nights at the Masque and Whisky A Go Go, where plentiful sweat, manic scrawled graffiti, and sizzling three-chord wonders held sway in 1978.

When punk burst through the nylon sheen of West Coast pop culture in the moribund mid-1970s, it flowed in multiple directions, from the turbo-charged, thorny, brash masculinity of Black Flag and the contagious, chaotic philosophical musings and musical disruption of the Germs to the keen, incisive social political observations of the Avengers and Dils. X went even further, grafting a whole history of music, tilted towards Americana, into its resilient fabric and injecting a poetic despair and bar-stool literary abandon into lowbrow rock 'n' roll.

"Punk rock was always about more than just music," Doe attested to me in 2013. "We believe in the power of all mediums to effect cultural change. In the earliest days, everyone expressed themselves in a variety of ways: art, clothing, attitude, philosophy, etc."

In fact, by 1982, the band had left the tag behind, preferring to think of themselves, as Exene told *Creem*, "A rock 'n' roll band . . . I think it's safe to return to that now. We've been waiting for the day when we finally would not have to be a punk band anymore" (qtd. in Grabel 40). Or, in some sense, they birthed through punk to a place where influences—from Jerry Lee Lewis

MUTANTS
MAY 11th

X — Hollywood/Los Angeles

ADMISSION: 3 BUCKS

9 P.M.

ALLEY CATS — Hollywood/Los Angeles

SYMPTOMS

863-9890

330 GROVE St. SF

The Vex calendar with Top Jimmy, the Unknowns, The Brat, and more, early 1980s.

Previous page: X, 330 Grove St., San Francisco, CA.

and Carl Perkins to Eddie Cochran and Scotty Moore, to the poet Bukowski, Dixieland, disco, the Doors, and Lead Belly—could be worn like a second skin, revitalized, recast, and reworked. This occurred just as their notion of punk was now more about "trying to make it not more sophisticated, but more effective," not affected (Grabel 17). This was a working band in stark contrast to labelmates the Eagles, and they were a band more enraptured of the Plugz, Top Jimmy (himself a well-received musical journeyman from Kentucky raised amid "country and hillbilly bluegrass"), and Phast Phreddie and Thee Precisions than to punk's scattershot squads.

Doing so meant they created something as tempered, emblematic, stylized, and enduring as Patti Smith but even more syncretic: they revisited the tin-can AM dreaminess of 1950s radio, borrowed a bit of dusty twang and chrome-lined rockabilly, vented anger like Vietnam era protestors, embraced the moody, eruptive Doors, and shook with buzzsaw but hummable punk. In essence, they created a series of albums that feel like *Heart of Darkness* set in a lurid, crumbling, shadowplay Los Angeles strewn with fragments of Charles Bukowski, Dashiell Hammett, Arthur Rimbaud, folk broadsides, teenage kicks, B-movies, sleazy tabloids, and the salt of the earth.

"There are always remnants of that past," Doe admits. "But many of the physical landmarks are gone. The soul of each city remains, San Francisco with a dark kind of spooky energy, [while] Los Angeles will always seem open, wild, and boundless. In Los Angeles, the light and horizon are mostly intact. The desert and ocean are still only moments away. All cities in the U.S. are undergoing a seismic shift."

X were an unparalleled force that made formerly "unheard music," lurid punk with doses of rockabilly and country twang, go viral in the days of watered-down college rock. In the middle of hardcore's buzz-haired scorn and FM radio leotard cock rock, X held their ground. They were ductile anchors as glam-metal reigned over Sunset Strip.

Doe's family helped carve that anchor, stir his eventual creative whorl, and plant his feet in music. "I remember my father playing piano around the house when we were at home and listening to classical music, which I will do on occasion, driving or something like that," remembered Doe when I interviewed him in Houston, when X opened for Blondie. "I think I also started listening to classical music through Charles Bukowski. He'd always write to it, but he's not so much of an influence anymore. Getting introduced to music happened through folk music, actually. My parents gave me my own records: folk music like Lead Belly, Woody Guthrie, and 'Cisco' Houston. One guy that my aunt actually knew was Sam Hinton, who was a marine biology teacher in San Diego, kind of a musicologist (who started the San Diego Folk Song Society). It was all stories and had the roots of music. These were the building blocks. . . . In X, we were all listening to country and western music, and I listened to a lot of blues and folk music. I began to think, these are all the same: these are the same chord changes. The melodies are simple, so let's bring some of that stuff in there. The Gun Club was certainly part of that. It wasn't like you needed permission. Billy was doing that stuff from the beginning. He was putting a Chuck Berry riff before 'Johnny Hit and Run Pauline' as a sort of wink to 'Johnny B. Goode.'"

In mid-2014, Yep Roc released the "part scrapbook, part roadmap" known as *The Best of John Doe*, which underscores his intelligence, earnestness, and songcraft rather than the fierce, feral, and barbed poetic license of his youth. In the eyes and aim of Doe, the messy politics of modern life has been replaced by, or perhaps internalized in a metaphoric tangle with, the interpersonal

X, Euphoria, Portland, OR, 1982.

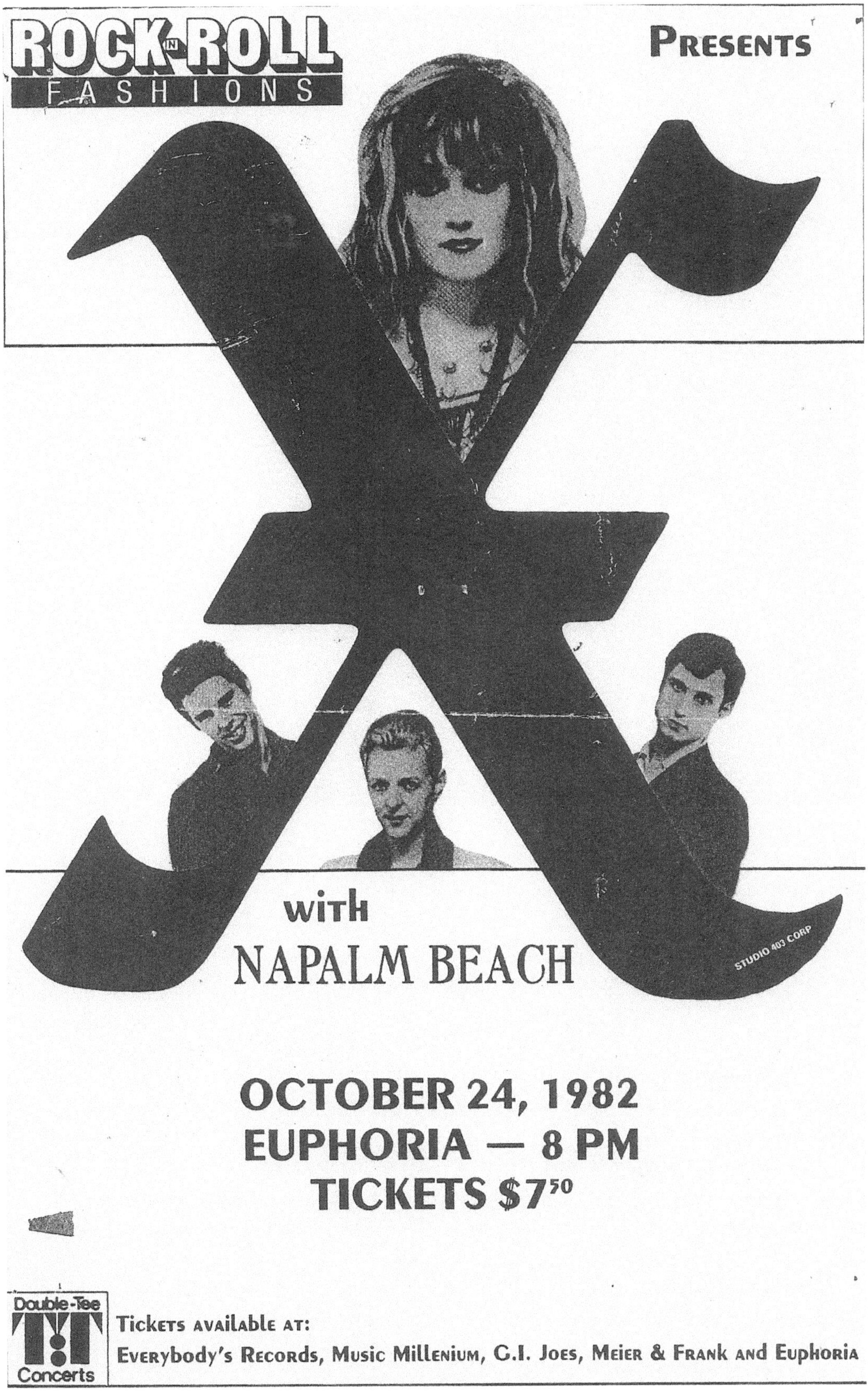

ROCK IN ROLL FASHIONS **PRESENTS**

X

with NAPALM BEACH

OCTOBER 24, 1982
EUPHORIA — 8 PM
TICKETS $7.50

Tickets available at:
Everybody's Records, Music Millenium, G.I. Joes, Meier & Frank and Euphoria

Billy Zoom, X, Heights Theater, Houston, TX, 2017, by David A. Ensminger.

politics of relationships stretching over years, places, and points of conflict. Men are not mere naked, hollow shells. They are lovers figuring out the terrain as the ground shifts underneath them. Love, desire, and loyalty rub elbows with disarray, aloneness (rather than loneliness), and botched duties.

But X itself continues as a potent band still on the live music circuit. However, they have become much more than an ornery, "loud fast rules" soundtrack to an aging crowd endowed with leftover ennui. They continue to offer a metaphoric undertow that is trans-generational: they still speak to the forgotten, ignored, and borderline miscreants, those lonely, roughed-up, and hardscrabble ones.

"We felt that connection, but it wasn't always returned," says Doe in 2015. "We've always been more popular in bigger, more free-thinking cities. Manufacturing left the U.S. in the '70s, and people are just now realizing what we gave away."

X albums exuded small flashes of Memphis soul, hard-churning rockabilly, 1930s dance tunes, country howls, punk vitriol, even disco-funk, but all were recognizably X. Yet, when asked, "Do you see yourself as a kind of ambassadors of American music?" Cervenka kept her response to my inquiry almost timid: "Well, we just write and played what we felt, and our influences were rock and roll, jazz, country, etc. People might see us as ambassadors now."

"We opened for X early on in our career in San Diego, in 1980," remembers Dave Alvin. "X were very picky about who played with them. By this time, they had just put out their first album. The first time I saw X they were the opening act for Arthur J. and the Gold Cups and Black Randy and the Metrosquad, then two and a half years later they were X. They were really picky, and we had somehow slipped onto the bill in the gig in San Diego. The promoter had seen us do a gig in San Diego at a bar for free beer, the Spirit Club. And she had a club where she did more hardcore punk like X, Dickies, and people like that. She really liked us and put us on the bill with X without checking with X. There was some trepidation on X's part, like 'Who are these guys, what the hell is this? They are a rockabilly band? Nobody is better than Billy at rockabilly.' We went up and did our thing and were great. We went over great with the audience, but more importantly, we went over well with X. So, then we soon opened for X at the Whisky."

In addition to being music world gatekeepers of a sort, X were a cultural phenomenon that mixed and matched end-of-the-century artistic attitudes by combining film noir alleyway luridness with deadpan writer Charles Bukowski vibes, or converged film threats like James Dean with a sense of savage motorcycle boot cool. Their narratives brimmed with jouissance, a jarring physicality: each song felt like a compressed tale oozing with drugs and booze, mirroring the engulfing world of glaring porn shops, burning trash cans, and dank clubs filled with graffiti.

Or, in the case of songs like "The Have Nots," they catalogued the scrappy world of working-class blues, the endless rundown bars that have disappeared. First they became dwarfed, then eliminated, by the Disney-fication of Los Angeles. That same sense of loss is pregnant with meaning in "The New World" too, which offers a lens panning across rust-belt America—Flint, Gary, Buffalo—and seemingly bemoans the evaporating culture of America in late-stage capitalism on the cuff of what has now become the attention economy, the era of robots and artificial intelligence, and the digital nexus.

X emblazoned such songs with narrative grit and granular detail about people, bars, cities, political vibes. The songs represent a map of loss "to some extent, which is why we were chronicling them," explains Cervenka. "We started touring when the manufacturing was being phased out, leading to the 'rust belt.' Sad to see. But many smaller cities have really recovered. People are staying in those places and making them vital again, so that's very good.

Exene Cervenka, X, by Edward Colver.

"You ask a lot about the people at that time," says Cervenka. "Yes, we were all nobodies and proud of it. The Midwest still had blue-collar cities and jobs, stockyards, breweries (not the fancy kind, the beer made in Milwaukee, St. Louis, East LA), and most kids had some hope and some kind of work they did to survive. Rents were cheap, cars were cheap, guitars and amps were cheap, and there was still an old-fashioned American way of life." Hence, hope has not entirely dimmed: those tour sites have begun rejuvenation.

Yet, the golden age of fanzine networks and college radio—so different in terms of both culture and economics—that gestated the band may be a mystery to a young person today. "I don't think it's possible to explain real freedom of that sort to people who have never experienced it," avows Cervenka.

"That's all we had, our bohemian life," Doe avows. "It also owes something to John Waters, Andy Warhol, Lou Reed, and the "sort of famous" celebrity that we all thought was wonderfully twisted, sarcastic, and poking fun of 'real' celebrity culture. If only people would be hip to that nowadays."

Cervenka continues: "I was thinking of all the celebs and rock stars and bands now who are in their early twenties, and how different their lives and goals are. It's either wealth and fame derived from sex or nothing it seems."

Their sense of America felt transgressive, forbidden, and alluring, like an algorithm of anarchic tendencies. Just note their record covers: their debut album from 1980 featuring an overlarge X burning furiously in the dense black night. When she is not singing, Cervenka has always been a pointed, offhand

DJ Bonebrake, Heights Theater, Houston, TX, 2017, by David A. Ensminger.

intellect with a knack for making pastiche-style, expressionistic journals and sculpting castoff material into punk folk-art that blends Hispanic traditions with her own wonky visions.

Doe's voice and complex persona have only deepened over the years. And X's recent touring with their original lineup, with adroit powerhouse DJ Bonebrake on drums and masterful Billy Zoom on sizzling guitar fretwork, always delivers the past as a silver dagger to slice through the muck of current music.

When I asked DJ about his own history and style, for instance if he painted a house to earn the money to buy a Ludwig marching snare he used in both a Buddhist marching band and the early X material (a snare so loud it cut through the noise at dingy clubs), he explained: "It was Nichiren Shoshu Buddhism. I was a member for about five years [1967–72]. They had a marching band and a big band. I started in the marching band but later graduated to the big band. I bought the Ludwig marching drum in about 1970 but later used it in the Eyes and then in X. It wasn't necessarily louder, but it was deeper sounding.

"I get bored easily," he admitted. "I've always played different styles of music and played in multiple bands. The period between 1978 and 1987 was the exception. I was playing almost exclusively with X during that period. When we started, the performers and the fans hung out. It was a small scene. A lot of the fans were or became performers. Our experience allowed us to be more pliable. We experimented and twisted the songs in the direction they needed to go. In 1988, when X took a break, I started freelancing with

X: Under the Big Black Moon

Billy Zoom, X, by Edward Colver.

various rock and pop bands and for fun joined a jazz band and a community orchestra. It was also the period I began studying percussion again: Murray Spivack (snare drum) and Dale Anderson (marimba and vibes). If you visit LA, chances are you'll see me around town playing in an Irish band, a jazz band, a blues band, a fusion band, a wedding band, a surf band, an orchestra, a salsa band, a rockabilly band, a country band, a bluegrass band, a folk band ... I'm sure I've left out a half dozen genres."

Still, as punk history becomes revised again and again, some aspects get whitewashed or go missing. I feel young writers don't understand the pivotal role of distinct personalities—radio personality Rodney on the ROQ, or punk visionaries like Chris D. of the Flesh Eaters, Darby Crash of the Germs, John Denney of the Weirdos, or Alice Bag of the Bags, or fanzine editor Claude Bessy, as well as Exene and John, and on and on. They imprinted their own pulsating uniqueness on the genre.

"I think the smaller details get left out," Cervenka reminded me. "Many people think hardcore and punk are the same, and that's kind of true, but the two were also at odds. Our scene is still kind of underground. It was a long time ago. Things get lost."

X, Liberty Lunch, Austin, TX, 1993, by Randy "Biscuit" Turner.

Hence, each song revisited by X on the stage every night to this day also becomes its own form of cultural recovery; the songs bristle with punk's initial promise to build an art that speaks to duress and intrigue, fiction and fury, real-life restlessness and agitation. They catalog the world as it once unfolded across scratched, dented vinyl albums, pregnant with their own darkness and redemption.

"Many song lyrics start off as poems," Doe says, "and are edited to fit into the meter of the song. We, like many other writers, simply write. Later on you figure out what it can be used for. Many of the lyrics to the first X songs started as poems, and most of them could be published as poems."

And each night they feel vital and candid, shored up by their pressing electric energies.

"Everyone was and is into music and scenes for different reasons," Doe suggests. "Even within the same band. It's a personal choice, but then people allowed for variety. Sadly, there will never be a time when the line, 'The world's a mess / it's in my kiss' or 'It was better before they voted for what's-his-name' doesn't apply. Also, the second verse of 'I Must Not Think Bad Thoughts' will always ring true."

X: Under the Big Black Moon   195

John Doe, Mucky Duck, Houston, TX, by David A. Ensminger.

"John is as down to earth as it gets," observes Tony Erba, noted and beloved hardcore singer from the Midwest who is also a tradesman by day. "Road-weary and wizened, but he *never* forgets where he came from, always pays homage to Darby and the Masque and the Weirdos scene. I feel he recognizes that he stumbled into something so original and organic and realizes that, even though with all his brilliance and charisma, it was that rarefied time in space in '77 LA that charted his course. Like AC/DC, he hasn't deviated much from his chosen path . . . he writes solely from the heart."

"It was all very political, and revolutionary," Cervenka, in turn, stresses. "A friend said to me recently, punk rockers would be considered potential domestic terrorists these days by the current regime. We had freedom, and I would rather have freedom than wealth and fame. Really, we had it all. And in many ways, hanging on so long, and still loving what we do, is the best life I could have hoped for."

If people are disappointed by Cervenka's embrace of conspiracy-minded thinking, maybe the truth was always hiding beneath the clothes, as Tequila Mockingbird, aforementioned singer and producer, notes: "Playing with X was always fun. Ray Manzarek was always around. He was a pal and a great guy. Everyone was cool, and we all got along fine. I have been sort of shocked by the

X, Nightlife, Austin, TX, by NOXX (Michael Nott), 1980s.

politics that have come up as of late. Before that, I never had any trouble with any of those people. X and the Blasters are still my friends, as far as I know.

"People become who they are. The roots part is actually what the Blasters and X are. Like, with X, when Exene made some money, she decided to settle down, so she moved to Idaho. Deep down inside, she had Republican leanings. People become their parents when they grow up. I didn't, but a lot of people do."

REFERENCES

Alvarado, Jimmy. Messages to the author. January/February 2021.
Alvin, Dave. Interview with the author. *Thirsty Ear*. 2000. Print.
Alvin, Dave. Interview with the author. February 2021.
"Black Flag." *Non-Stop Banter* 1, no. 4 (November–December 1985). Print.
Blocher, Karen Funk. "The Clash/Bonds." *Relix* 8, no. 4 (August 1981). Print.
"Blood on the Saddle." *Last Rites* 8. Print.
Bonomo, Joe. "The night AC/DC stormed CBGB." *Salon*. November 4, 2017. Web. https://www.salon.com/2017/11/04/the-night-acdc-stormed-cbgb/. Accessed January 16, 2019.
Brown, Glyn. "Scorched: Jason and the Scorchers." *Sounds*. May 25, 1985. Print.
Buj, Otto. "Big Chief." *Sold Out* 9. Print.
Carnes, Kevin. Interview with the author. *Houston Press*. July 8, 2015. https://www.houstonpress.com/music/the-bristling-activism-behind-kevin-carnes-relentless-beat-7568640.
Case, Peter. Interview with the author. *Left of the Dial* 1. 2001. Print.
Case, Peter. Interview with the author. *Left of the Dial* 8. 2004. Print.
Case, Peter. Interview with the author. March 2021.
Case, Wendy. Interview with the author. *Left of the Dial* 3. 2002. Print.
Chable, Christopher Alex. "Guerrero, Eduardo 'Lalo'" (1916–2005)." *Celebrating Latino Folklore: An Encyclopedia of Cultural Traditions, vol. 1*. Ed. Maria Herrera-Sobek. ABC-CLIO. 2012. Google Books. Accessed January 20, 2021.
Chandler, John. "The Replacements, December 7, 1985. U of O, Oregon." *Puncture* 11.
"Chasing the Meat Puppets." *Jet Lag*. December 1985. Print.
Cosloy, Gerard. "Bring On the Jerks." *Boston Rocker* 30. 1982. Print.
"The Cramps: Voodoo Rockabilly." *Chic*. July 1984. Print.
"Cuts." *New Vinyl Times* 2, no. 2. Print.
Daniel, Drew. "How to Act Like Darby Crash." *Listen Again: A Momentary History of Pop Music*, ed. Eric Weisbard. Duke University Press, 2007. Google Books. Accessed December 30, 2020.
Darling, Cary. "Wall of Voodoo." *Trouser Press*. January 1983. Print.
Dean, Edward. "Screamin' Sirens." *Band Age* 2. 1987. Print.
Demorest, Stephen. "Punk Rock and the Sex Pistols." *Hit Parader*. October 1977. Print.
Dictor, Dave. Interview with the author. February 2021.
Doe, John. Interview with the author, in David Ensminger, *Mavericks: Conversations with Artists Who Shaped Indie and Roots Music*. Rowman and Littlefield, 2014. Print.
Doe, John. Interview with the author. *Houston Press*. January 23, 2015. https://www.houstonpress.com/music/john-doe-makes-it-easy-to-root-for-the-underdog-6775195
Dunhill, S. "Local Releases." *Terminal Mind* 8, 1982. Print.
The Enigma Variations. LP, Enigma Records, 1985.
'Enthal, Andrea. "Tex and the Horseheads." *Spin*. June 1985. Print.

Erba, Tony. Messages to the author. January 2021.

Escovedo, Alejandro. Interview with the author. *Thirsty Ear*. 2000. Print.

Farber, Jim. "The Ramones: Too Punk to Pop!" *Hard Rock Video* 7. April 1986. Print.

Floyd, Gary. Interview with the author. *Left of the Dial* 1. 2001. Print.

Floyd, Gary. Interview with the author. February 2021.

Floyd, Gary. *Please Bee Nice: My Life Up 'Til Now*. Left of the Dial, 2014. Print.

Foley, Michael. Interview with the author. *Houston Press*. December 22, 2015. https://www.houstonpress.com/music/creative-crimes-revisiting-dead-kennedys-apocalyptic-punk-masterpiece-8013787.

Gilbey, Ryan. "Kink, drink and liberty: a queer history of King's Cross in the 1980s." *The Guardian*, May 16, 2017. https://www.theguardian.com/stage/2017/may/16/queer-history-kings-cross-lgbt-80s-london. Accessed March 16, 2021.

Gimarc, George. *Post Punk Diary: 1980–1982*. St. Martin's Griffin, 1997. Print.

Gira, M. Interview with the author. *Left of the Dial* 2. 2002. Print.

Goldstein, Toby. "Shooting Stars: Patti Smith." *Grooves*. 1978. Print.

Gordon, Keith. "Burning a Hole: Jason and the Scorchers." *East Village Eye*. August 1984. Print.

Grabel, Richard. "X's Wild Los Angeles Gift: Sign on the Dotted Line, Please!" *Creem*, June 1982. Print.

Green, Jim. "Green Circles." *Trouser Press* 86. June 1983. Print.

Hildado, Melissa. "Gente from La Puente: Brown, Queer, Underground Punk Icon Shines the Light on Those at the Fringe." *KCET.org*. February 18, 2021. Web. https://www.kcet.org/shows/artbound/gente-from-la-puente. Accessed February 19, 2021.

Hill, Michael. "Force of Impact: Black Flag Assess the Damaged." *NY Rocker*. May 1982. Print.

Jones, David. Messages to the author. January/February 2021.

Jones, Texacala. Interview with the author. February 2021.

Joseph, Lee. Interview with the author. *Left of the Dial* 5. Winter 2003. Print.

Kinman, Chip. Interview with author. *Modern Machines*. Left of the Dial. 2020. Print.

Kinman, Chip. Messages to the author. January 2021.

Kinman, Tony. Interview with the author. *Left of the Dial* 3. 2002. Print.

Klein, Howie. "Interview with the Clash." *Search and Destroy* 6. Print.

Klein, Howie. "Interview with the Clash." *Search and Destroy* 7. Print.

Kokinis, Troy. "'The Sky Is Black and the Asphalt Blue': Placing El Monte in the Early LA Punk Scene." *Tropics of Meta*. April 22, 2014. Web. https://tropicsofmeta.com/2014/04/22/the-sky-is-black-and-the-asphalt-blue-placing-el-monte-in-the-early-la-punk-scene/. Accessed February 19, 2021.

LaFemina, Gerry. Email letter to the author. February 2, 2021.

Lopez, Robert. Interview with the author. *Left of the Dial* 3. 2002. Print.

Lopez, Robert. Interview with the author. January 2022.

MacKaye, Ian. Interview with the author. *Left of the Dial* 1. 2001. Print.

Magrann, Mike. Email to the author. March 4, 2021.

Marshall, James. "Country Punk: A Hound's Eye View." *East Village Eye*. August 1984. Print.

McMahon, James. "Melancholia and raw pain: the sad end of Leatherface." *The Guardian*. November 6, 2015. Web. https://www.theguardian.com/music/musicblog/2015/nov/06/

melancholia-and-raw-pain-sad-end-leatherface-dickie-hammond-frankie-stubbs. Accessed January 21, 2021.

Miller, Chris. "Music." *Playboy*. December 1973. Print.

Mockingbird, Tequila. Interview with the author. June 29, 2021.

Morris, Keith, and Jim Ruland. *My Damage: The Story of a Punk Rock Survivor*. De Capo Press, 2016. Print.

"Music." *Playboy*. February 1977. Print.

"Music." *Playboy*. June 1977. Print.

"Music." *Playboy*. September 1977. Print.

Needs, Kris. *Dream Baby Dream: Suicide, a New York City Story*. Omnibus, 2017.

Nellis, Barbara. "Fast Tracks." *Playboy*. May 1981. Print.

Nelson, Chris. "The Cramps Have This Thing About Elvis." mtv.com. August 15, 1997. Web. http://www.mtv.com/news/920/the-cramps-have-this-thing-about-elvis/. Accessed December 30, 2020.

"New York Dolls." *Teen*. Reprinted in *Ripped and Clipped* 4. Print.

"Nick Cave Gives . . ." *Sounds*. May 25, 1985. Print.

Oliver, Myrna. "Jeffrey Lee Pierce; Leader of Gun Club Rock Band." *Latimes.com*. April 2, 1996. Web. https://www.latimes.com/archives/la-xpm-1996-04-02-mn-53944-story.html.

Playboy. November 1987. Print.

Porter, Dick. *Journey to the Centre of the Cramps*. Omnibus, 2015. Google Books. Accessed December 30, 2020.

Powers, Kid Congo. "Hollywood Punks Presente!" *Razorcake* 79. 2014. Print.

Priewe, Marc. "Resistance Without Borders: Shifting Cultural Politics in Chicana/o Narratives." In *Re-Framing the Transnational Turn in American Studies*, ed. Winfried Fluck, Donald E. Pease, and John Carlos Rowe. Dartmouth University Press, 2011. Print.

Rake, Jamie. "Scream: This Side Up." *Sound Review* 5. Summer 1986. Print.

"Reviews." *Playboy*. July 1983. Print.

Reynolds. Simon. Interview with the author. *Popmatters*. November 27, 2011. Web. https://www.popmatters.com/151683-simon-reynolds-redux-a-conversation-from-the-past-about-post-punk-2495914373.html.

Ringenberg, Jason. Interview with the author. *Left of the Dial* 1. 2001. Print.

Robinson, Lisa. "Fast Talking and Instant Recognition with the Clash." *Hit Parader*. September 1980. Print.

Roessler, Kira. Interview with the author, in David Ensminger, *Left of the Dial: Conversations with Punk Icons*. PM Press. 2013. Print.

Sachs, Lloyd. "Music." *Playboy*. April 1983. Print.

Salewicz, Chris. "The Clash Play Revolution Rock." *Trouser Press*. March 1980. Print.

Salewicz, Chris. *Redemption Song: The Ballad of Joe Strummer*. Faber and Faber, 2006. Google Books. Accessed January 3, 2019.

Schwartz, Andy. "The Dils Disband." *New York Rocker*. May 1980. Print.

"Scream." *Ink Disease* 4. 1983.

Shaw, Greg. "Independent America." *New York Rocker*. May 1982. Print.

Shredder. "Phast Phred." *Flipside* 38. 1982. Print.

Smith, Jeff. Email to the author.

Smith, Jeff. Interview with the author, in David Ensminger, *Austin Punk Invasion: A Collection of Interviews, Art, and Reflections*. Left of the Dial. 2018. Print.

Smith, Jeff. Message to the author. April 11, 2022.

Stark, James. *Punk '77*. Self-published. 1992. Print.

Stegall, Tim. "Stuck Inside Samoa with the Punk Rock Blues Again." *Jet Lag* 80. December/January 1988. Print.

Stein, Julie. "Swinging Possums." *Punk Globe*. January 1982. Print.

Stirling, P. "Camper Van Beethoven live review." *Puncture* 11. 1986. Print.

Thrasher, Glen. "Hickoids: We're in It for the Corn." *Sound Choice*. Summer 1986. Print.

TSOL. Interview with the author. *Left of the Dial* 1. 2000. Print.

Turner, Gregg. Interview with the author. *Left of the Dial* 1. 2000 Print.

Vale, V. "Interview with the Dead Kennedy's." *Search and Destroy* 9. 1978. Print.

Vez, El. Interview with the author. *Left of the Dial* 2. 2002. Print.

Watt, Mike. Email to the author. January 4, 2019.

Wheeler, Drew. "Jason and the Scorchers." *Creem*. October 1984. Print.

Wilkins, D. A. "Husker Du." *Local Anesthetic* 17. 1982. Print.

Willman, Chris. "X profile." *BAM*. September 9, 1983. Print.

X. Interview with the author. *Houston Press*. April 15, 2015. https://www.houstonpress.com/music/a-lively-round-table-with-the-still-dangerous-x-7373178.

X. Interview with the author. *Houston Press*. May 2, 2019.

X.U. "Gun Club live review." *Hymnal* 2. Print.

Yohannon, Tim. *Prison Bound* review. *Maximum RocknRoll*. June 1988. Print.

Young, Charles M. "Frankenchrist." *Playboy*. March 1986. Print.

Young, Charles M. Young. "The Sex Pistols in Texas." *Rolling Stone*. February 23, 1978. Print.

Young, Jon. "Alan Vega: Saturn Strip." *Trouser Press*. March 1980. Print.

Young, Jon. "Cross Their Hearts: The Lords of the New Church Bring the Bad News to America." *Trouser Press*. January 1983. Print.

Young, Jon. "Plimsouls: Everywhere At Once." *Trouser Press*. March 1980. Print.

Young, Jon. "Outside the Bands Don't Toe the Line." *Trouser Press*. February 1981. Print.

Young, Jon. "Robert Gordon." *Trouser Press*. March 1980. Print.

Younger, Rob. Interview with the author. *Left of the Dial* 7. Winter 2004. Print.

Zimmerman, Kent, and Keith Zimmerman. *Sing My Way Home: Voices of the New American Roots Rock*. Backbeat Books, 2004. Google Books. Accessed January 4, 2019.

Zollo, Paul. "Happy Birthday Peter Case: A Celebration of the Long Goodbye." *American Songwriter*. March 2021. https://americansongwriter.com/happy-birthday-peter-case-a-celebration-of-the-long-good-time/. Accessed June 29, 2021.

INDEX

AC/DC, 9, 196, 199
Adkins, Hasil, 31, 51
Agent Orange, 19
Alice Cooper, 19
Alvarado, Jimmy, 99–101
Alvin, Dave, 13, 31–44, 94, 101, 102, 124, 165, 191
Angry Samoans, 6–7, 9
Ash Grove, 32–34, 94
Austin, Texas, 24, 38, 55, 67–68, 70, 72–73, 77–78, 80, 88, 108, 129, 133–34, 153–56, 175–76
Avengers, the, 19, 154–55, 185

Bag, Alice, 60, 157, 194
Beach Boys, 20
Beatles, the, 20, 62, 67, 79, 137, 144
Beatnigs, the, 179–84
Benally, Jeneda, 25–26
Biafra, Jello, 3, 84
Big Beat Records, 6
Big Boys, 47, 68, 72, 84, 85
Black Flag, 7, 10, 38, 54, 64, 84, 89, 115, 166, 167, 185
Blood on the Saddle, 40, 112
Bonebreak, DJ, 193–94
Bowie, David, 16, 20, 123
Bragg, Billy, 86, 184
Buffalo, New York, 137–40, 151, 191
Bukowski, Charles, 188, 191
Byrds, the, 20

Campi, Ray, 31, 33, 37, 154
Canned Heat, 36, 69
Carnes, Kevin, 179–84
Carter Family, 133
Case, Peter, 50–51, 91–93, 102–3, 137–52

Case, Wendy, 24–25
Cash, Johnny, 4, 21, 29, 155
Castration Squad, 7
Cave, Nick, 48, 53, 121, 173
CBGB, 25, 85
Cervenka, Exene, 103, 185–87, 192, 194, 198
Channel 3, 13–16, 20
Charles, Ray, 37
Chicago, Illinois, 44, 79, 125, 138, 181
Chocolate Watch Band, 6, 9
Circle Jerks, 7, 19, 89
City Lights Bookstore, 144
Clash, the, 14–15, 16–17, 37, 40, 48, 66, 84, 155
Cochran, Eddie, 47, 187
Coltrane, John, 108, 125, 159, 168
Costello, Elvis, 4–5, 33, 154
Cowboy Nation, 10, 136
Cramps, the, 50–54, 111, 120
Creedence Clearwater Revival, 14, 40, 167
Creem, 24, 185
Crime, 31, 35, 145
Crypt Records, 6
Cynics, the, 6

Dash Rip Rock, 29
Davis, Miles, 42
Dead Boys, 26, 85
Dead Kennedys, 3, 9, 48, 65–66, 84, 181
Deadbeats, the, 60
Desjardins, Chris, 101, 102–4, 119–28, 165
Deville, Mink, 33, 37, 146
Dickies, the, 5, 34, 38, 85, 191
Dictators, the, 9
Dictor, Dave, 54–56, 77–88

203

Dils, the, 10, 19, 38, 40, 47, 129, 131, 134, 145, 154, 185
D.O.A., 166, 183
Doe, John, 19, 24, 124, 136, 185–98
Donovan, 20, 143
Doors, the, 19, 187
Dos, 10
Downey, California, 31–32, 36, 94, 165
Dream Syndicate, 42, 121
Dylan, Bob, 19–20, 22, 79–80, 96, 103, 138, 143, 146, 148

Earle, Steve, 31
Eater, 5, 19
El Vez (Robert Lopéz), 45–64, 157
Ely, Joe, 37
Emory, Ron, 5
Erba, Tony, 24, 196
Erickson, Roky, 9, 124
Escovedo, Alejandro, 25, 40, 102, 129, 131, 144, 153–58

Fear, 7, 38, 40, 85, 89
Feathers, Charlie, 31
Flesh Eaters, 40, 89, 101, 111, 119–27
Flipside, 47, 94
Floyd, Gary, 65–76, 82, 84–85, 153
Foley, Michael Stewart, 9–10
Fuzztones, 6

Gears, the, 98, 101
Germs, the, 6, 13, 107, 145, 185, 194
Get Hip Records, 6
Ginsberg, Allen, 143, 150
Go-Go's, the, 5, 7, 41, 104, 107
Gordon, Robert, 33
Gories, the, 6
Government Issue, 19
Green, Al, 123, 127
Green on Red, 40, 115, 121
Grand Ole Opry, 69
Grateful Dead, 20, 79–80, 143
Grisham, Jack, 5
Guardian, The, 16, 48

Gun Club, 51, 66, 89–106, 111, 115, 119, 121, 188
Guthrie, Woody, 26, 53, 79, 188

Haggard, Merle, 131
Harman, James, 33–34, 38
Hendrix, Jimi, 19–20, 66, 172
Hite, Bob, 36
Holly, Buddy, 134
Hooker, John Lee, 48, 69, 127
Hopkins, Lightnin', 32–33, 37, 42, 69, 127, 151
Hurt, Mississippi John, 36, 137

Idol, Billy, 45

Jackson, Joe, 5
Jason and the Scorchers, 20–23
Jones, David, 60–61, 98, 103
Jones, Elvin, 168
Jones, George, 40, 101
Joseph, Lee, 6
Joy Division, 19, 101

Kaa, Jim, 20
Killing Joke, 5
Kinman, Chip, 38, 46–47, 129, 130–33
Kinman, Tony, 10, 38, 129, 134, 154
Knitters, the, 107, 185

LaFemina, Gerry, 25
Lalo, Don, 60–61
Lead Belly, 96, 138, 146, 187–88
Levi and the Rockats, 31, 34, 115
Lewis, Jerry Lee, 19, 130, 185
Little Richard, 55, 130
Long Beach, California, 33, 50, 148, 165
Long Ryders, 40, 42
Los Angeles, California, 4, 6, 19, 22, 34, 42, 60, 90, 93, 97, 112, 116–17, 119, 125, 129, 143, 159–60, 168, 188, 191
Los Lobos, 13, 31, 38, 40, 57, 60
Lynn, Loretta, 115
Lyres, 6

Mabuhay Gardens, 34–35, 144–45
MacKay, Ian, 51, 84–85
Magrann, Mike, 13–16
Marsh, Dave, 31
MC5, 6, 9, 72, 143, 153, 181
MDC, 54, 56, 66, 77–80, 82, 86–88, 183
Meat Puppets, 13, 111
Midnight Records, 6
Minutemen, 9, 159–68
Mockingbird, Tequila, 6–7, 105, 196–97
Monkeys, the, 19
Morrison, Jim, 19, 106

Nelson, Willie, 69, 78, 88, 133
New Wave Theatre, 7, 105
New York, New York, 4, 22, 87, 129, 151, 154
New York Dolls, 6–7, 9, 22, 47, 79, 123
New York Times, 9
Nuns, the, 129, 144–45, 153–56

Owens, Buck, 69

Pandoras, the, 6
Pere Ubu, 146, 154
Perkins, Carl, 21, 40, 187
Pettibon, Raymond, 162, 168
Plimsouls, the, 41, 93, 103, 141, 142, 146, 148, 149
Plugz, the, 6, 38, 103, 107, 141, 146, 187
Pogues, the, 14, 16, 151
Pop, Iggy, 72, 162
Posy Boy Records, 14
Presley, Elvis, 45–50, 53–63
Punk Globe, 12–13
Pure Hell, 19

Radio Birdman, 4
Ramones, 9–10, 21–22, 24, 26–27, 48, 51, 57, 72, 82, 85, 97, 118, 146, 148, 175
Rank and File, 10, 13, 40, 71, 129–37
Replacements, the, 20
Reynolds, Simon, 17–19
Richman, Jonathan, 6
Ringenberg, Jason, 20–24

Riverside, California, 6
Robbins, Ira, 65
Roessler, Kira, 10–11
Rolling Stone, 16, 23, 41, 88
Rolling Stones, 16, 19, 57, 96, 123
Roxy Music, 97, 156
Rush, Otis, 38
Ruts, the, 19

Sahm, Doug, 138, 176
Salewicz, Chris, 16
San Francisco, California, 10, 34, 48, 54, 56, 65, 82, 85, 140, 143–45, 155, 179, 187–88
San Gabriel Valley, California, 89–90
San Pedro, California, 159, 163, 165
Saturday Night Live, 7
Scream, 16–17, 19
Screamers, 13, 34, 145
Search and Destroy, 10, 17
Sha Na Na, 7
Sinatra, Nancy, 19
Sister Double Happiness, 66, 75–76
Slash, 34, 89, 91, 101, 124
Slash Records, 13, 40, 42, 103, 131
Smith, Jeff, 27, 171–77
Smith, Patti, 19, 27, 45, 82, 84, 97, 115, 121, 124, 144, 187
Social Distortion, 19, 29
Sound Choice, 16
Standells, the, 19
Stiff Little Fingers, 5, 19
Stooges, the, 6, 9, 21, 72, 123, 154, 156, 159–60, 162–63
Swinging Possums, 10, 13

T. Rex, 167
Taylor, Gene, 36
Terry, Sonny, 140
Thee Midniters, 90, 97, 102
Top Jimmy, 113–14, 187
Toxic Reasons, 19, 54
Troggs, the, 6, 19
Trouser Press, 3, 65, 129
True Believers, 153, 175

Turner, Gregg, 7–9
Turner, Randy "Biscuit," 55, 68, 72–73, 85, 99, 195
Turner, Tina, 69
Twisted Roots, 10, 13

Van Morrison, 140
Velvet Underground, 6, 9, 19, 123, 134
Vincent, Gene, 45
Voxx Records, 6

Waters, Muddy, 40, 127
Watt, Mike, 4, 50, 159–70, 176
Weirdos, the, 20, 38, 145, 194, 196
Whisky A Go Go, 38, 185, 191
Who, the, 129–30, 154, 171
Wild Seeds, 175
Williams, Hank, Sr., 21, 22, 24, 37, 40
Wilson, Jackie, 34
Wire, 19

Younger, Rob, 4

X (the band), 185–98

ABOUT THE AUTHOR

David A. Ensminger is a college instructor of English, humanities, and folklore in Texas; a drummer with decades behind the kit; an author of several books covering both American roots music and punk rock history; and an ongoing contributor to magazines in America and Europe. His research has been highlighted in *The Economist* and the *Boston Globe*.

www.ingramcontent.com/pod-product-compliance
Lightning Source LLC
Chambersburg PA
CBHW041238240426
43661CB00071B/2918